Dedicated to the memory of great Aunty Baddy (Emma Harrison) who proved that you're never too old to be converted to the Boro cause, making her Riverside debut at the grand old age of 100 years young. Also to our mam and dad and everyone who has suffered for this labour of love called *Fly Me To The Moon*. I can't forget to mention the very people who make this Boro thing so special, Boro fans everywhere, long let the Boro bug continue.

First published in Great Britain by
Juniper Publishing, Juniper House
3, Sandy Lane, Melling, Liverpool L31 1EJ
Fax & telephone 0151 531 8506
1999

Copyright FMTTM 1999

The right of FMTTM to be identified as the
authors of this book has been asserted by them
in accordance with Copyright, Designs and
Patents Act 1988

All rights reserved. No part of this book may be
reproduced in any form or by any means
electronic or mechanical, including
photocopying, recording or by any informational
storage and retrieval system without the
permission, in writing, of the publishers.

ISBN 09528622 4 7

Reprographics:
P's and Q's Ltd., Unit 10 Gibraltar Row,
King Edward Industrial Estate, Liverpool L3 7HJ

Printed and bound by:
Albion Graphics, Old Connelly Complex,
Kirkby Bank Road, Knowsley Industrial
Park North, Kirkby, Merseyside L33 7SY

FMTTM
was written in lunar modules

Sort of edited by

Robert (Shrug) Nichols

Layout

Stephen Bickham (the best)
Rob Nichols (the rest)
Sharon Caddell (almost)

Front cover

Norton Design

Produced by a rapidly ageing

John Wilson

Credits: Bob Fischer, Chris Bartley, Ian Nesbitt, Stuart Downing, Miniature G, David Shayler, Ian Cusack, Harry Pearson, Nick Varley, Mike Baker, Jonathan Todd, Simon Bolton, Geoff Vickers, Andy Smith, Mark Coupe, Rob Hymer, Dave Johnson (Rav's Rant), Robbie Boal, Alex Wilson, Mark Drury, Cory Muzyka.

Cartoonary: Andy Bland, Davey Roofus, Dave Bailey, Nigel (Camsell's dad) Downing, Andy Gillandi Schmultz.

Snappers: Tim Hetherington (Mogga etc), Paul Thompson (Hickton, Hendrie), Alex Wilson (Gary Gill, Boro Thru the Ages) Brian Spencer

Editorial

Hey we finally made it. I can hardly believe it. Yes we've made it into hardy perannual format at last, Alan Titchmarsh would be so proud. Out there with the big boys and there are still column inches to spare before the end of the millennium. I guess it has to be the realisation of something of a dream for many who have served time in the Fly Me crew. Since the early hurly burly days when it all began at the dog end of the eighties skipper Andy Gillandi, Stuart (Miniature G) Downing and his brother Nigel (Camsell's Dad/Endy) Downing have all harboured thoughts of shelf space next to the Beano, Dandy and Blue Peter annuals. But how could we be so bold when the curse of Fly Me was still hanging ominously in the air? You remember the curse don't you? You know whenever we branched out from the fanzine straight and narrow we were immediately shot down by that fickle finger of fate. Look at our t-shirt back catalogue of errors, Slaven for Scotland and he instead opts for Ireland, Pears - Ripe for the Picking and injury against Grimsby forced him to withdraw from the England B squad. Then there was the Rioch ZDS Final t-shirt, need I say more?

Then one fine spring morning through the portals of the stately Moon Towers boxroom office stepped our knight in shining ... v-necked plum-coloured jumper, Mr John Wilson with his promise to sign, seal and deliver our most coveted dream and put us up there on the golden shelves of bookshops the length and breadth of err.... Teesside and beyond. Fortunately John and his Juniper bush of publications had not got wind of the curse of Fly Me and so we just about got away with it, several computer hitches and glitches later. And here we are.

You may well be all a quiver wondering what delights there are in store for you as you journey through this A4 monstrosity. Well stop being so lazy and look for yourself. You'll find no contents guide short cut here, you can pick your own way through this wordy mire. It would hardly be right for me to make it easy for you, after all there ain't nothing easy about being a Boro fan. We make no apologies for the nostalgia bias of this our first foot forward into hard back. We want to wallow in the oh-so-nearly successes and glorious failures that have made us into the battle-hardened Boro fans that we are. Yet it's not all hysterical historical for we also get our crystal balls out, well why not, it's Christmas after all? We penetrate the dense fogs and smogs that shroud the future to seek out what twists and turns the next millennium will hold in store. If you hadn't guessed already there will be plenty of mileage left in the rollercoaster ride that is Boro. Don't you just love it! It's not just for Christmas Boro is for life.

So dust down those Boro tinted spectacles, nestle back in a comfy chair and let your fingers do the walking through this very first Fly Me To The Moon annual. We'll see you in the next Millennium.

Come on Boro!

Robert (Shrug) Nichols

The Eddie Holliday Story

Fly Me To The Moon's intrepid investigative reporter Perry Raylor lifts the lid once more on the tragedy that rocked north eastern football in the fifties and he has a damned good rake around while he's at it too.

Look in your Harry Glasper and you'll find Eddie Holliday's name between two other Middlesbrough heroes David Hodgson and Walter Holmes. Read the pen pic notes and there's a description of one of Boro's all time greats. A speedy left winger, Holliday fired many of the bullets for our dynamite strikeforce of Clough and Peacock to wreak havoc on opposition defences. Holliday's club successes were rewarded with three full caps for England. In all he played 169 first team games for Boro in two spells between 1956 and 1966. But behind the star-burst statistics there lurks an altogether darker side. For Eddie Holliday nursed a problem and this is his shocking story as it was first told to me many years ago. Memory may have muddied a few details but I think it went something like this.

Holliday was first spotted in unusual circumstances by Boro director Charles Amer. Back in the summer season of 1956 young Eddie was working as a red coat at Butlin's Holiday Camp, Filey. Coincidentally Boro director Charles Amer had just been appointed Camp Entertainments Officer. Amer joined a crowd of holidaymakers as they watched a football match between the redcoats and the Butlins inmates. He was so impressed by the aptly named Holliday's rapier-like wing play, that he immediately contacted Boro boss Bob Dennison, who offered Eddie a two-week trial at Ayresome Park. Eddie Holliday sailed through his trial and within only a matter of weeks of joining he was absolutely flying in the first team.

Yet there was a second string to Holliday's bow, being a redcoat he had to entertain the campers on an evening as well as a daytime. Down in the ballroom Eddie Holliday was the business. He could dance, he could act, he was a demon with the jokes and he could even pass off the odd conjuring trick. Eddie's real talent however lay with the microphone, fronting the house orchestra he had no peer. Billed as the crooners crooner Holliday had a voice to curl up and die for. Charles Amer ever a shrewd judge for a bargain thought he had struck gold. He had a real double whammy on his hands. For as well as signing Holliday for his football team the wily operator immediately snapped him up to sing with his dance band. Amer it was who renamed his young protégé to avoid any confusion with another famous Edward, dance band leader Edward Heath. From now it was to be Eddie Holliday by day and Billie Holliday by night. And so a legend was born.

The Barnsley born baritone couldn't believe his luck, plucked from relative obscurity he was suddenly a star in two separate walks of life. His weekends were a veritable whirl of excitement, an away match at Doncaster Rovers would be followed by an omnibus to woo an expectant dancehall at the Rotherham Apollo. He might share a football field with notable team mates including Clough, Peacock, Day and Ronnie Dicks, then on the evening he could be rubbing shoulders with the likes of Joe Loss, Max Jaffa and the king of light entertainment himself, Dickie Henderson. Few would not have envied a glamorous lifestyle spent in Bradford B&Bs, Grimsby greasy spoons and Leeds lodging houses.

Sadly after a couple of years this double life began to take its inevitable toll. His footballing form suffered as he suffered from over-exhaustion. In truth he had difficulty cramming in enough rest between matinees and matchdays. His schedule was so hectic that he had to grab forty winks wherever he was, whether in a boarding house or in a third class compartment of the Flying Scotsman. It was a nightclub owner in Pontefract's paradise strip who innocently proffered what proved to be fatal advice to Holliday. "Always take a little something to help you get your head down, love." Holliday followed the tried and tested WMC remedy and found it worked for him, yes sleep came all the easier with that little nightcap or nosegay to send him off. But unfortunately all too soon he was starting to build up a real dependency. Holliday was now never seen without his telltale hip flask. Indeed things got so bad that he was once ordered from the field of play to remove his flask. Apparently in his notes to the FA, referee Arthur Ellis related that, and I quote, "I was becoming increasingly concerned that Holliday's vessel would interfere with me' dipstick." It might easily have been a knock-out blow.

A worried manager Bob Dennison ordered Holliday to take a well-earned .... rest (you thought I was going to say holiday, didn't you?). But a holiday was the last thing "Billie" needed, you see away from the strictures of training and the disciplined lifestyle of the honed athlete he could now indulge himself to the limit. And beyond. His particular poison was not whiskey, vodka or gin. Hideous as it is to relate "Billie" Holliday was overdosing on Ovaltine. England's number one ovaltini was now reduced to a near permanent catatonic state. The unfortunate Holliday imbibed more and more and quickly withdrew into his shell (the vast amount of calcium he was now taking in caused rapid growth of fingernails and bones. The accusation by team-mate Alan Peacock that Billie had no spine could not have been further from the truth).

The end makes tragic reading. Middlesbrough trainer Harold Shepherdson was dispatched to accompany the winger/singer back to Middlesbrough but discovered Holliday slumped in a chair in his Rhyll chalet. In his evidence at the inquest Shep described opening the holiday chalet and being immediately aware of, "that unmistakable odour of cocoa." Shep knew at once that he had uncovered a terrible tragedy. "Everywhere I looked there were empty cans of Ovaltine. Poor "Billie", he just didn't stand a chance."

And that ladies and gentlemen is the sobering, extremely tall tale of Eddie "Billie" Holliday. And a final word of warning from this cautionary tale, the next time someone says to you "I should cocoa," tell them to think again, drink tea, coffee, orange, coke or lemonade but never ever, ever abuse the brown stuff.

Future Perry Raylor investigations will unearth some of the other great mysteries that stalk football folklore. Perry poses the real questions others refuse to ask. He asks was Mel Nurse a nurse? Did John Wark prefer to walk? Is Ian Bishop a real Bishop? Is Robbie Savage so savage? If this is up your street, crescent or back alley then please keep on turning these pages. There's far more complete twaddle and hoddle to come. Mmm.... yes please!!

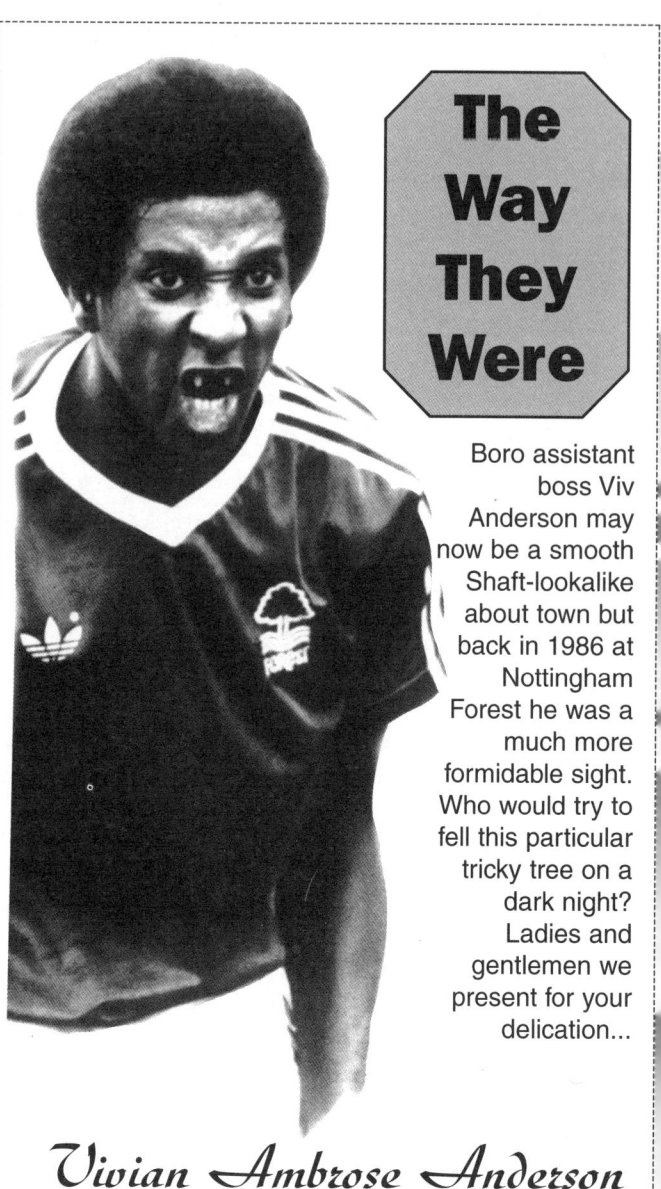

The Way They Were

Boro assistant boss Viv Anderson may now be a smooth Shaft-lookalike about town but back in 1986 at Nottingham Forest he was a much more formidable sight. Who would try to fell this particular tricky tree on a dark night? Ladies and gentlemen we present for your delication...

Vivian Ambrose Anderson

Moonlighting as **the afro count**

The FMTTM Millannual

The FMTTM Millannual

THE SECRET DIARY OF CRAIG SUMMERDALE AGED 20 AND A QUARTER

TUESDAY 31st AUGUST 1999

Well! Here we are! I must admit, dear diary, I've never actually KEPT a diary before, and I only got the idea yesterday when I accidentally stumbled across Mr Stamp's secret pantry (where he keeps his secret pants) underneath the South Stand. I was looking for the Little Boys Room (as opposed to the Big Boys Room where Mr Deane and Mr Festa go) and I wandered through a large metal door with "PRIVATE! DANGER! KEEP OUT!" stencilled upon it. Inside I found Mr Stamp sitting on a large golden throne surrounded by empty crisp packets and bottles of Sunny Delight.

"Eh fella!" he shouted to me as I peeped around the door jamb. "What's the matter, can't you read?"

"No," I replied, truthfully. "I'm only 20 and a quarter and Mr Robson says I have to be at least 25 before I'm allowed to read properly otherwise I might take a proper look at my contract and start getting funny ideas. I couldn't even tell you what it says on that book there..."

And resting on the floor next to a pile of Cadbury's Fuses and a Mr Kipling's Bramley Fancy was a battered blue exercise book. "PHILIP STAMP'S SECRET DIARY" it said on the front in big black marker pen.

"That?" said Mr Stamp, "Eh now, that's where I keep all me secret thoughts like, all me deepest darkest innermost ruminations on life that combine to create an all-encompassing philosophy and, some might say, almost a design for living in an era of pre-millennial angst and uncertainty..."

And so I picked it up and had a flick through, but all the pages were blank! Well, I thought to myself almost straight away, I'm sure I can do better than that...

Anyway dear diary, allow me to introduce myself. My name is Craig Summerdale, Boro junior at your service, my all-time ambition is to make the big grown-up first team and on TV this morning I had one of the nicest things in the world happen to me! No, not Sian Lloyd presenting the weather in leather trousers (although believe me, that did make me feel a BIT funny) but Mr Robson, yes THE Mr Robson on the local news saying that I might be allowed to make the bench this weekend! Well dear diary, I immediately tore off my "Super Boro" Robbie Mustoe print jim-jams (he's my hero) and raced down to the Brilliant BT Super Cellnet Ripping Riverside Stadium as fast as my little legs could carry me. Unfortunately though, as soon as I walked into Mr Robson's office I got into rather a lot of trouble. This was for two main reasons...

1. In my excitement, I had forgotton to replace my "Super Boro" Robbie Mustoe print jim-jams (he's STILL my hero) with any OTHER clothes. The only person allowed to strut around the Brilliant BT Super Cellnet Ripping Riverside Stadium COMPLETELY naked is Christian Zeige (he's a member of what Mr McQueen calls a "poncy German Naturist Club". Apparently they have nearly 30,000 active members all over the Black Forest) and so I have been fined a week's wages. Gosh! £75 down the drain just like that!

2. I seem to have misunderstood the cut of Mr Robson's jib. "I'd like to ask about making the bench" I said to him. "I've got to admit I've got a couple of queries..."

"So did we, but we sold them at the end of last season!" guffawed Mr McQueen, who was standing nearby ironing his shorts. It must be quite an unforgiving place where he comes from because everybody else I know takes them off first.

"I'd just like to ask about the tracksuit." I said. "Will I need to buy my own because I can't really afford it with me being on free school meals and everything..."

Mr Robson looked at me quizzically then led me without a word to the very edge of the Riverside Stadium pitch where all the big grown up players play.

"When I said you'd be making the bench this weekend" he explained, "I think you might have got the wrong end of the stick..." and he showed me to a wheelbarrow containing six planks of wood, a bag of nails, a stepstool, a stillsaw and a hammer. "The plans for the bench are in there too" he said, angrily. "And let's hope your carpentry's a bit better than your tackling or no doubt it'll collapse ten minutes into the game!" And with that he gave me a playful cuff in the testicles and wandered back to watch Home and Away. One day, dear diary though, one day...

Love, Craig xxx

The Curse of the Boro Supporters Club

By the end of the 1999/2000 season, the Boro Supporters Club will have reached a milestone; it will be ten years old. I'm speaking here about the current Supporters Club, being well aware that the original organisation was in existence for considerably longer than a decade. The present group was formed in the later stages of the 1989/90 season and we're still going strong today. Of the original committee line up only our current Chairman, David Buckton has stayed the course, the original cast included one Rob Nichols, and I wonder what ever happened to him?

Over the years, we've had some great times and some truly memorable guests have entertained and informed us. One of the most popular get-togethers has always been the Player of the Year Awards Night, when fans and players have gathered to witness the presentation of our annual award, voted for by Supporters Club members nationwide. However, despite the popularity of the event, players may no longer be too keen to lift the award, as a recent analysis of past winners and their subsequent fortunes at the club makes pretty torrid reading. Rumours of a curse upon the award may not be totally without foundation. Maybe you should decide for yourself. So here to help you make your mind up I present to you the full list of winners, but please be warned these tales of woe are indeed very spooky.

1990/91 - Ian Baird: always a popular lad during his short spell at the club was Bairdy, so it was no surprise when he picked up the first ever trophy. Yet within months he was plying his trade at Hearts and we never saw the trophy again.

1991/92 - Stephen Pears: what a season for Pearsie, who only missed out on an England place after a freak cheekbone injury. Upon hearing of the accolade of being our Player of the Year, he promptly suffered a major injury to his knee, missed the promotion game at Wolves and half of the following season.

1992/93 - John Hendrie: one of the few bright spots following relegation was hearing that Hendo had signed a new contract after rumours of his possible transfer had been rife. John collected our trophy and began the next season well - until he was injured and missed about four months of the remainder.

1993/94 - Curtis Fleming: a solid season for Curtis rewarded with the Supporters Club honour, which he was well chuffed to receive. Sadly he hadn't checked on what was happening to previous winners and suffered a major injury that kept him out for most of the following season.

1994/95 - Derek Whyte: Deggsy didn't actually pick up his award until well into the next season, which might explain why things were still going OK for him up until that point. No sooner was the trophy in his hands however, then loss of form and persistent subs bench warming ensued.

1995/96 - Steve Vickers: Steve picked up just about every award going this season but maybe should have steered well clear of ours. He didn't too badly the following year but lost his place towards the end of the season as his form dipped alarmingly.

1996/97 - Juninho: it was a never to be forgotten night. May 13th 1997 and the Ayresome Park pub was packed to the rafters to witness the little genius collect an award that his name on it right from the very start of the season. The tears flowed as everyone acknowledged that our hero was soon to be leaving us. That he did too, but not without carrying the curse along with him. The 1997/98 season saw him suffer a broken leg, the loss of his Brazilian national team place and the end of his World Cup dreams and eventually even his place in the starting line up at Atletico. Now he could be on his way back to us - the final stage of the curse perhaps!

1997/98 - Gianluca Festa: our one and only success story, with the Italian having proved mighty resistant to the power of the curse. Luca only just missed out on reclaiming the trophy last season, something no one else has ever come close to achieving - not that they would want to after reading this.

1998/99 - Hamilton Ricard and **Robbie Mustoe:** so, what's in store for these two? The curse would have to have grown some to bring down both of them together but do not doubt it's power. Robbie demonstrated a slight loss of form in the early season and is no longer a constant starter in midfield. Not the best of years to pick for a Testimonial perhaps. As for Ham, he's been OK so far. Let's just hope that we're still saying that at the end of the season.

Come April or May next year, we'll be presenting the award for the current season. Given the history of the trophy, it may well be a prize that no one wants to bag. Or is there anyone out there who has the power to reverse the curse.

Simon the Wanderer

JACKIE CARR (1920s)
Jackie Carr a local lad,
A player sent from heaven,
From promotion sides to England caps,
Still playing at 37.

The FMTTM Millannual

BORO 2020

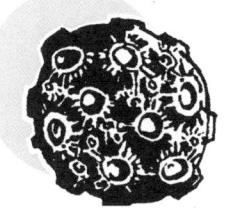

Well, here we are at the back end of 1999 and all of us here in the FMTTM office can't wait to see the Millennium. That's right, we'd rather spend all our time in dodgy nightclubs on Teesside Park than actually do any work, but the other day our esteemed editor R. Nichols Esq was heard approaching an anonymous FMTTM contributor and asking "So, Miniature G, what do you make of all this Y2K fever?"

"To be honest Rob, I prefer Brut 33 myself" replied the lad himself, but it didn't half get us thinking. Which is a novelty in itself in THIS office. With a century's worth of Boro fun now BEHIND us, what on Earth will things be like in the future? Well, if the past 100 years' worth of roller-coaster riding is anything to go by, there can surely only be one possible answer. Bloody awful. Still, with one hand on his crystal ball (hence his poor eyesight) and the other making arcane mystical movements in the air (two fingers raised) **BOB FISCHER** takes a look far, far into the future as FMTTM brings you... BORO 2020... (screen goes all wobbly)

Managed by 52-year-old ex-Boro hero **Fabrizio Ravanelli,** Middlesbrough have gone from strength to strength in recent seasons. Ravanelli, on his controversial return to the club in 2004, won over suspicous Boro fans by scoring 57 goals in the 04/05 season to gift Boro the Premiership Championship by February. His partnership with fellow striker Phil Whelan (sensationally converted to a forward by Oxford United and subsequently re-signed by then Boro boss Viv Anderson for £12.5m, Whelan went on to claim the Golden Boot in England's World Cup Winning Campaign of 2006) was voted by Boro fans as the clubs best ever. Ravanelli went on to coach the Boro youth team before eventually working his way up through the ranks and taking over as manager in 2010. His five-times-champions side includes...

KYLE HIGNETT: Signed as a youngster by his father Craig (Boro caretaker manager for six months in 2009 following Viv Anderson's dismissal for being "too silly"), Kyle has stayed to prove himself as a lynchpin in Boro's side. At 6'9", Kyle is superbly built to handle Boro's goalkeeping duties, and has gone on to prove himself an able successor to the veteran Ben Roberts. Although Hignett senior, cementing his reputation as the "new Brian Clough", once commented on his son's burgeoning success, "Aye, he might not be in danger of getting dropped at the Boro but if he doesn't tidy his bedroom at home I'll drop him off the edge of a bloody cliff". Higgy Snr has since gone on to win the European Champions League twice in a row with his all-conquering young Crewe Alexandra side.

MICHAEL OWEN: At the age of 39, Boro's maverick genius is continuing to silence his doubters with the occasional flash of on-the-field inspiration. With his "nightmare years" apparently behind him (a seven-year haitus at Juventus and Celtic was dogged by constant rumours of drinking binges, gambling, and womanising as Owen's "perfect" marriage to Sporty Spice disintegrated. Sporty went on to marry Jamie Carragher. Followed by Robbie Fowler. Then Vegard Heggem. Jan Molby. Etc) "Mazza" signed for Boro in 2018 and was placed on a strict fitness regime by Ravanelli to slim down from an astonishing 25-stone bulk. Despite having retired from International football before his 22nd birthday (on the eve of Kevin Keegan's disastrous 2002 World Cup campaign. 6-1 to the Faroe Islands. Honestly.) recent Premiership performances against Rushden and Diamonds and Burnley have led to renewed "OWEN FOR ENGLAND" calls in the daily green-top tabloids. Under-fire England boss Ruud Gullit insists "The door ish alwaysh open for Michael, if only he can prove he'sh in shhhhhape."

VD-4U: Since the turn of the millennium, android technology has revolutionised many aspects of human endeavour, not least of all of them, football. In 2010, clubs realised that rather than spend a fortune on human players, cybernetic technology had advanced to such a stage that it was now possible to produce top-flight robot footballers for less than £150. By 2012 every Premiership club had a Computer Cyborg Relations Officer prominent in its backroom staff, and Manchester United caused a sensation by becoming the first club in the world to field 11 android players in a cup-tie against Everton, including secret late-90s prototype Jaap Stam. After this, FIFA clamped down on the practice and now each club is limited to fielding only two non-organic team members at any one time. VD-4U was designed and built by Boro's veteran cybernetics expert Peter Creamer, and is a Mark XIII central defender model with built-in man-marking facilities. Unfortunately after a particularly heavy downpour at home to Stockport County, Ravanelli conceded VD was looking "a little rusty".

EMPEROR ZOD: With the discovery in 2017 of a multitude of intelligent life teeming throughout the solar system, Ravanelli and Boro instantly created football history by swooping for Uranus's highly-rated midfield general, Emperor Zod. Initially hampered in Premiership football by his elaborate Uranisian head-dress and flowing robes, after an inspirational pre-season pep-talk from Ravanelli himself ("Take off the elaborate Uranisian head-dress and the flowing robes"), Zod has proved himself indispensable, instantly winning over Boro fans with a superb Urbankan Podracer Laser Assault on Sheffield Wednesday's unpopular manager Carlton Palmer. And Boro's forthcoming interplanetary cuptie against Zod's former teammates on Uranus seems to have fired him up more than ever. "ZOD IT!!!" ran the Evening Gazette headline in January 2020. "I'LL STICK IT UP URANUS VOWS BORO'S ALIEN ACE". Many fans are already speaking of him as a potential future manager.

ROBBIE MUSTOE: Yes, at the age of 51, Robbie is still very much the engine room of Boro's midfield. His trademark bald head and flowing white beard have made him a cult figure in the Premiership, but since new FIFA President Vinnie Jones made the two-footed, studs-up, 30-yard-run-up and ten-minutes-late tackle not only legal but actually COMPULSORY in World Football, Robbie has certainly come into his own. Not a bad achievement for a man of his age. Following a bright start to the season, Robbie was instantly rewarded with a new 30-year Boro contract, but a sending-off in the next game for an overly-fair and well-timed challenge on Leeds United's robot striker 4U-2P (a tackle described by Ravanelli after the match as "Too poofy - a disgrace") has seen him suspended from football for a year... AND forced to miss a match.

Yes, after constant complaints from English football chiefs about the number of games being played, the Premiership season now takes place over the course of 15 years, a change made possible by advances in cryogenic freezing. Supporters organisations are, of course, up in arms about the prospect of players earning up to £250,000 a week for spending 9 months of the year in suspended animation - mind you, that never stopped Gazza in the 90s. Ho ho!

ALAN MOORE: Still here. Somewhere.

So there we have it. There's no place like home... there's no place like home... there's no place like home... (screen goes all wobbly again and Fischer wakes up in bed at home with a scarecrow, a fussy tin robot and a rather effeminate lion. Just a normal Saturday morning, then) A glimpse into the future, a small window on the shape of things to come (triangular) and a glimmer of hope for Boro fans everywhere. And as for Robbo in the year 2020? Where will HE be? Come on, be serious. 24-hour pubs have been open since the year 2002...

G-R-E-A-T BORO MOMENTS

JOHN HICKTON

"The Legendary Penalty Run-Up"

Hickton was the hero for a whole generation of local youngsters. At a time when Boro were a permanent fixture in the second flight it was John Hickton's shooting boots that put the pride into Teesside. Top scorer for six consecutive seasons, Hickton was quite simply a sensational striker.

Big John is remembered by many for his dynamic penalty kicks. Alastair Brownlee reckons that Boro's number nine started his penalty run ups from Albert Park gates but Fly Me To The Moon has unearthed evidence that it was an altogther longer affair.

and in a packed programme tonight....
Bob Fischer cuts snippets of genius from the Boro's match programmes of yesteryear

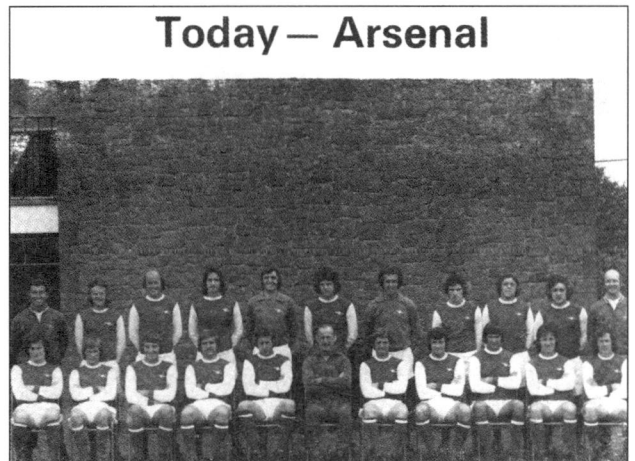

1976: ARSENAL'S DEFENSIVE WALL
The 28th of February 1976, and unfortunately a magnificent unbroken view of prime mid-seventies stone cladding has been semi-obscured by a raggle-taggle collection of hairy, flairy Arsenal players. Who took this photo? What on Earth were they thinking of? Were Arsenal secretly sponsored by Rimmer and Son Bespoke Stonemasons of Highbury at the time, or was it a primitive George Lucas blue screen technique to be filled in at a later date with spectacular special effects? Only one man has the answer. That's right, back row, third from the left - Terry Nutkins.

MOONSTRUCK
ALEX WILSON

Fly: YOUR FIRST GAME?
AW: Feb 1962 - Middlesbrough 1 Swansea 3. Joe Livingstone scored the Boro goal and I was the only one cheering.
Fly: Why?
AW: Cos' everybody else had left by then (getting beaten 3-0). Thirteen thousand people were there to enjoy it. So if I remember rightly there was Bob Appleby in goal, and I think there was Mick McNeill, Derek Stonehouse, Ray Yeomen, Ken Thompson (he's dead now God rest him but he was the player who got a life ban for accepting bribes when he was playing for Hartlepool a few year's later about the same time as Kay and Swan). There was Billy Day, Arthur Kaye, Joe Livingstone, Bill Harris and Eddie Holliday just before he got sold to Sheffield Wednesday. Two England internationals in that team, a Welsh international and yet we got stuffed by Swansea. I remember the headline the following day in the Evening Gazette, Cliff Mitchell, "Boro Hit Rock Bottom." I've never forgotten it. But we ended up twelfth that season so not so bad. We had a late surge after we signed Ian Gibson and he was the player who made the real difference. Not that I can remember much about it because my nose was up to the level of the Holgate wall. I was about eight at the time. They used to come around and shout at you for sitting on the wall. "Can't sit there son. Can't park there. No. More than my job's worth to let you sit on that wall." The early day's stewards.
Fly: YOUR BEST BORO MEMORY?
AW: Probably a match I didn't go to because I was away at school, the 4-1 Oxford win, to get us out of the Third Division. I stayed up to listen to it on the radio illegally. You weren't allowed radios at the school I was at.
Other than that, beating Newcastle or Liverpool in the Coca Cola. Just before Emmo left I said to him what is your best memory of Teesside. He said "The parties." I said, well after the parties. He said "beating the Geordies."
Fly: WHAT IS YOUR WORST MEMORY.
AW: Knowing the inevitable that we were going to get relegated with that team with Juninho, Ravanelli and Emerson. You could see it coming and despite the fact that in theory we could have stayed up on the last day, watching it in the pub, knowing that it wasn't going to happen. Just sinking slowly and slowly and slowly and even with Juninho's goal and seeing the little fella running around and trying to rally everybody and then sinking onto the pitch at the end. I thought there's a lot of people responsible but he's not one of them. That's what went through my mind on the day.

# of mags

by **Mike Baker**

The other day, I was browsing through some very old back issues of FMTTM, in a desperate attempt to cull from the archives some shred of inspiration for a Millannual article.

Sad I know, but the truth of it was I'd spent a week without cigarettes, and the abstinence was sending my brain in several different directions at once, all leading to surreal episodes where peoples' words became twisted into nicotine-related terminology (e.g. 'That'll be Embassy No. Six pounds fifty, please'; 'Fags very much').

Enough of that load of old Marlboro Light. These back issues were actually quite ancient; my oldest dated back to the time of Bruce Rioch, Zenith Data Systems Cup Finals and Ian Baird as Holgate hero. In those days, Mark Burke was talked of as if he was the next Lee Sharpe (this was 1989/90!), a campaign was started to have Bernie Slaven sent to Italia 90 as part of the Scotland World Cup team (he went, of course, with Ireland, and was amazingly overlooked in favour of legends like Tony Cascarino), and value for money at Ayresome Park was a hot and contentious issue (tickets were daylight robbery at £4 a pop!!!).

In any case, the piece that really caught my eye centred around the qualities that constituted

a true Boro fan.

The general consensus held that authentic fandom was wholly connected with actually going to matches. Back then, this was an opinion adhered to across the country. Football was still in the throes of a siege mentality helped along by the hysteria that followed Hillsborough, with its ID cards, mystical hordes of drunken hooligans and Ken Bates' electrically charged fences. I was a student living in Lancaster, only able to go to the odd match, or to away fixtures at crappy little grounds like Ewood Park, or Burnden Park's 'Asda End'. Coverage of football was in an entirely different universe to that offered now. Satellite television, in its pre-Premier days, could show the odd live match; otherwise ITV's The Match was the only place to be, with its spicy combination of Elton Welsby, Saint and Greavsie and blanket coverage of your team (as long as 'your team' was one of Manchester United, Liverpool or Arsenal). Newspapers were little better; sports supplements in broadsheets like The Times were things of the future, and football coverage was tucked neatly behind the financial pages. In short, keeping in touch with the Boro wasn't easy. A steady stream of FMTTMs sent from home was about all that kept me from being entirely excluded from the world of Ayresome.

In the current environment, it is difficult to appreciate the truth of the above sentence, harder still to contemplate the importance of fanzines in the last ten years when it comes to assessing the way football is perceived. It is a widely held belief that soccer's upsurge in popularity can almost wholly be attributed to England's success in the 1990 World Cup,

The FMTTM Millannual

but to agree with this would be to undermine the fanzine revolution.

At that time, FMTTM looked somewhat different to the edition you're reading now. Quality was not an issue; indeed it seemed that the scruffier a 'zine looked, the better. Desk top publishing was a computer-less concept; Cut & Paste involved scissors and Prit Stik. And yet, in a way, this was entirely the point. Match day programmes were glossy but sterile, whilst the Evening Gazette was so far up the club's behind that all reports carried an element of MFC approval that reached almost Soviet proportions in their lack of criticism. The gap for a fans' mouthpiece was wide open, and FMTTM filled it. Suffering from rough production those fledgling issues might have been, but as a cottage industry they held more value than all the officially approved literature in the world.

Beyond the letters pages of magazines and newspapers, the voice of the supporter had never been heard. Suddenly, club policy over matters such as pricing, transfer dealings and club improvements were open to criticism on a new level, and went far beyond the traditional channel of complaints, which involved booing the team as it left the pitch.

It must be borne in mind how far the image of the typical fan has developed in the last decade.

Ten years ago, the idea of the man taking his entire family to the match was virtually unknown;

believe the Government, and your snapshot of a typical terrace would be that of a vast pigpen bursting with small-minded thugs looking for a fight and running on lager. Fanzines altered this; their sheer articulacy confounded the popular opinion of supporters' intelligence. Clubs reacted in different ways to this new threat. Some, claiming that fanzine sales undercut those of official programmes banned sellers from their ground. Others, such as Manchester City in the early days of Francis Lee's regime, went so far as inviting the editor of King of the Kippax onto the Board, ostensibly to garner the views of the spectator, more clearly as a marketing stunt to curry favour with volatile fans. Most clubs turned a blind eye to their small-time critics; there was little they could do to stop people from selling copies, so they didn't even try.

The fanzine culture appears to have grown as far as it can, that it has finally reached a saturation point. Last year, FMTTM reported how few new writers have emerged in recent times, whilst many of the people originally involved in fanzines have moved on to bigger things,

such as Jim White (Darren Tackle in The Guardian) and Middlesbrough Supporters South's very own Harry Pearson. The presence of FMTTM within the Boro culture is now as accepted as that of post-Christmas slumps and defeats against Everton. There is a danger that far from being the radical organ of criticism and dissent of its early years, that FMTTM is now part of the brickwork, that it has become so established it is part of the establishment itself. And that idea holds some sense of truth; for me and many others, FMTTM

➤

15

◀ is central to the Middlesbrough experience. Something would be missing were it no longer there. What is more apparent is the upturn in the fanzine's quality, the advent of glossy covers and higher production values have run parallel with the improved standing of the club itself. Like the daddy of fanzines - When Saturday Comes - FMTTM has been able to gradually drag itself from its roots to become what it is today, a thriving concern in its own right. The crucial point is that the spirit has never really altered. FMTTM is still a vessel for the comments and criticism of fans everywhere, and is never afraid to take cheap shots at rival clubs, something I always expected to see more of in the programme (you know the kind of thing I mean: Today, we welcome our illustrious local rivals, Ruud Gullit's Newcastle... doesn't fully capture the sting of a heated derby atmosphere).

It is only very recently that I've learned to appreciate the importance FMTTM still has on my supporting life. Since graduating from University, I've stayed in the north-west and have been forced to worship the Boro from some distance. I no longer subscribe to this chauvinistic notion that real fans are those who go to matches; like many who stood on the Holgate in the immediate post-liquidation years, I can't help wondering where these new supporters have sprung up from. Besides which, I am more or less priced out of putting in personal appearances. Objecting to

The Internet has quite possibly become my best and most important source of Middlesbrough facts and gossip. Whereas in the past I would have to trawl through Ceefax or buy a paper, these days virtually everything I want to know is available at a mouse-click on the right bookmark.

The coverage on SKY Sports is about as good as it is ever going to get. Far removed from the bad old days, the knowledge that you will get to see your team at least three times during the season is a comforting one. At last, we have a televisual medium that can offer the amount of football coverage the public demands. I am in complete sympathy with those who argue against having to pay extra for the peoples' game, but there are no terrestrial alternatives that could provide this amount of viewing for the armchair fan. Sadly, recent murmurings suggest that televised football is about to hit the pockets further, with the introduction of matches on a pay-per-view basis, but at present, the small monthly payments for this much football represents a happy and affordable medium, especially to those who cannot go to games. Newspaper reporting has improved immeasurably; the introduction of Fantasy Football leagues seems to be a telling factor in this. The media have also introduced a number of magazines for adults, infiltrating a football market only served by the likes of Shoot! and Match not so long ago. Four Four Two might scream 'Coffee table!' at those with the taste not to buy it, but its importance cannot be underestimated as a barometer of the market now open to football-related literature.

The identity of the supporter has altered in ten years to the extent that we have transformed into a nationwide supportage; ten years ago, you would never have heard politicians declare their allegiance to certain teams, nor read reports about France 98 from such luminaries as Martin Amis or Melvyn Bragg. At the turn of the millennium, supporting a club from afar is easy, in fact almost too easy. I have noticed more and more how the reportage I have easy access to has a septic whiff about it. These media speak from the point of view of the national, uninformed football fan; you can see it in the way they still dish out the old jibes about Boro (such as gags about wantaway Brazilians in a recent Observer). In fact, they know nothing about the club, nothing about being a lifelong supporter, appreciating the tension a 5-0 defeat against Everton engenders despite being over a hundred miles away from its epicentre. This truth never fully occurred to me until I received the later editions of FMTTM from the last season. The negative vibes provoked by the last season could only be appreciated from the contents therein, the letters, editorials and comments. On the surface of it, 1998/99 appeared an impressive campaign, resulting in our best finish for 20 years. It should have seemed that this was good enough, but it wasn't, and fans of the club reported why not to a degree, and with

shelling out for something that has risen 500% in price since 1990 should be reason enough for not going, but the fact is that I just can't afford it.

a passion I would never have gleaned from the dailies.

It seemed that despite all the impressively modern methods in which I could summon facts and stats about my team, the only way to get to the real core, to the feelings of those who appeared to struggle alongside Middlesbrough during every reverse, after every PR disaster, was to read the fanzine, still the only effective channel for the supporter wishing to share the mood with other supporters.

This, surely, is the real relevance of FMTTM.
There is no point pretending that it can comment on footballing developments on an even keel with professional journalists; it can't. What it continues to do is provide the fan's point of view. Ultimately, Boro must carry a degree of answerability to its fans; without this element the vital link between a club and its community would be severed and football would have little remaining significance. For me, FMTTM provides a service unique from other communication channels, it lets me know the word on the terraces, the feelings from those who matter. It has become something of a beacon to supporters, a focal point for criticism of Middlesbrough FC, a reminder that in the end, wherever we live and however many matches we are able to go to, we are united in our support for the club and all its culpability.

G-R-E-A-T BORO MOMENTS

ARCHIE STEPHENS- HANGS IN THE AIR

Signed from Bristol Rovers in March 1985, Archie "Hatchet" Stephens sixteen league goals in the Third Division Promotion Season of 86-87 set Boro well on the way to recovery from liquidation. Most of them were thundering headers to which Archie's ability to "hang in the air" contributed greatly - a feat which our 1999 Hatchet model demonstrates here with great aplomb. Geddin!

players in the moon - ARCHIE STEPHENS

FIRST GAME

Charlton away and the home game me and Brian Laws joined we were given sponsored cars on the pitch. We were the only players to get good cars, the other players all got small Astras we got Cavaliers.

Fly: Looking back in the reference book I see that the crowd was only about 5000.
Yes. But those 5000 were the loyal ones. I'd hate to see what would happen now if anything happened here what would the crowd go down to now? But there's that much money in the game now the club needs to stick where they are don't they?

LAST GAME

It was early in the season after we got promotion to the First Division. It began OK against Millwall. It was one all and I scored with one of those headers. I thought I'd be there for that season. Then I had Kernaghan wanting to take over from me. Bruce called me in to see him and said there would be competition for places and Kernaghan's going to be competing for your place, I thought Kernaghan wasn't good enough to lace my boots and I told Bruce that. Obviously Bruce did and he said Carlisle are interested, I knew the manager Clive Middlemass from my Bristol days. He said do you want to speak to him and I knew then that I was out of the door, although he didn't force me. But I went to Carlisle and I think it was the worst move I made.

BORO BODIES

The Boro players are losing their heads. I've heard people talk about headless chicken but this is ridiculous. Can you please wag a helping hand in the general direction of the Middlesbrough players past and present and liberate them from their present head-masters. Just who is it running out under the lovely locks of the very bonny Ms Gail Porter? Damon Albarn's practising his Beetlebum but what a cheek it's not even his own. Danni Mingoue looks like she's gone all anipodean with her sponsors but just whose shirt is she wearing down under? Hmmm's got me stumped. And I was the one who put the thing together. never mind I've written the answers down upside down at the end. But don't cheat, now...

The answers my friend are blowing in the wind of change - but in case you didn't guess them all.

1. Gail Porter is astride her Scottish compatriot the living leg-end Bernie Slaven.
2. Whose that with the cheeky wiggle Mr Albarn? Why that'll be that nice Master Colin Cooper.
3. Well yes of course Scary Mel is hitching a ride on Jan Aage's aero-plot.
4. Jamie Pollock's never looked more demure than when he's wearing Danni Minogue's beautiful block and tackle. Yes he looked kind of familiar didn't he?
5. Jenny Powell is admiring the view from the the very fine pair of shoulders of our cool Colombian kiddo Hamilton Ricard.
6. And finally the one you struggled with. Right Ted. That'll be Andy Townsend there Ted .... Oh feck.

Marooned on Moon Island

WE DUMP DAVE ROBERTS (SKY SPORTS/MAGIC FM) ON THE DESERT ISLAND OF THE MOON AND ASK HIM SOME QUESTIONS.

WHICH 5 BORO MATCH VIDEOS DO YOU WISH YOU'D TAKEN?
MAYBE YOU WOULD LIKE TO LISTEN TO SOME RADIO COMMENTARIES AS WELL, MAYBE.

1 Juninho vid - when I'm p*ssed off I still slap it in, it cheers me up even if The Mags and Makems win!
2 My Coca Cola Cup Final TFM commentary tape with Big Jack - just reminds me that I wasn't dreaming... WE WERE THERE!!!!!
3 Liverpool v Boro v Liverpool - Both CCC Semi Final - All I remember was that I p*ssed myself when McManaman took his shirt off to give it to Baker and then I simply went apeshit at the CRS!
4 Match of the Day (1975) - When 'Big Chin Hill' thanked the Boro fan who'd sent in a road map to show them the way to Ayresome Park. It's the only time ever when his face was a picture.
5 A recording of 'Sportstalk' an LWT (Tyne Tees of London) programme I did a week before FA Cup Final as a studio guest. Whilst live on-air I stopped the show to put a Boro shirt on the FA Cup - yes handles in the arms and pointy lid through the neck 'n everything. Littlewoods went bezerk and told LWT they'd never ever have the cup again.

WHICH BORO MEMORABILIA WOULD YOU HAVE TAKEN WITH YOU? TELL ME.

My 'Players and Officials Only' sign from above the Ayresome players entrance - yes I bought it in the auction.
My picture of the Wembley scoreboard 5 mins from time in the CCCFinal saying - Boro 1 Leicester City 0.... it's on my website.... and the patio set Higgy gave me when he left for Aberdeen.... you know something soft to park me arse on and drink the coconut juice.

WHICH STRIP DO YOU WANT TO KEEP YOU WARM?

The 70's away one - you know the Blue & Black vertical stripes..... just loved it.

WHICH BORO PERSON WOULD YOU WANT TO KEEP YOU COMPANY?

Big Jack cos he pulls no punches - I could listen to him for hours. At half-time on the TFM Cup Final commentary I asked him about the Ireland rumour that he pays for drinks over there with a cheque which never get cashed 'cos the barmen always frame them and put them on the wall - his reply on the radio - "Bollocks! I really hate that story. It makes me look like a right tight sod!"
The other would be me old mate Higgy - He's just hyper. He can't stop - a typical scouser always talking, messing about. He can't stop.... he'd be ideal 'cos he's non stop entertainment.

TELL ME YOUR BEST BORO MEMORY, NOW.

Rav's Wembley goal..... as near to Premier Event Ejeculation as I've ever got! The other was being in the Holgate End goal for a half time penalty shoot out at Ayresome when Boro were playing Newcastle in a testimonial game..... Kevin Keegan walked over to watch and was duly greeted with a chorus of "It 'im on the 'ed with a baseball bat, Keegan!" We offered him the ball to take 3.... the first whizzed into the top corner..... the second sent me the wrong way.... and just before he hit the third a booming voice came from behind, "For f**k's sake keeper save one. You're sh*te. Sadly I only managed to get a finger to it but thought afterwards how well the Boro lads handle the English language.

AND WHAT ABOUT YOUR ...WORST MEMORY?

Emile Heskey's equaliser..... that definitely cost us both cups, Europe and the Premier League.... of that I'm certain. It was even worse than Rav and Emmo walking out.

AS A YOUNG CHILD WHO WAS YOU FAVOURITE BORO PLAYER?

Jim Platt, as I was a goalkeeper on the Boro's trainee books as a lad you know!

WHAT WAS YOUR FIRST BORO GAME? TIME TO TELL ME.

Oxford at home Jan 24th 1969 - Boro won 2-0 Crossan and Hickton -23,030..... mind you I had to ask me Mam! (Laughs)

THANKYOU AND GOODBYE DAVE!

The FMTTM Millannual

19th century

by Rob Shrug

Roll on the new century, good riddance to this 20th century charade.

Middlesbrough fans will have that extra special reason to welcome in the 21st century. I'll tell you why, the twentieth century has done this football club of ours no favours whatsoever. In fact the past hundred years has been an age of adversity, it has been a real milieu of mediocrity. But I reckon that we have been merely experiencing what you might describe in football parlance as a blip, or a hiccup. Start a fresh in the virgin territory of a brand new century and you watch us go. We'll swing right back into top gear at once, carrying on from where we left off in the good old 1800s. Just watch the shelves of that trophy cabinet buckle and break under all the weight of the silverware.

History doesn't lie but Middlesbrough have been lying asleep. Compare our records over the two centuries of our history.

Formed in 1876 we were well ahead of all the southern clubs, still a mere twinkle in a public schoolboy's eye at that stage. In 1881 a Cleveland side, including five Middlesbrough players blitzed a combined Northumberland and Durham team by ten goals to nil. That's right we knocked TEN past a combined Sunderland and Newcastle team. We were absolutely unbeatable in the north-east. Boro had even defeated two of Glasgow's finest sides Govan and Athole a few months before, and everyone was raving about the Scots players at this time. We were indisputably Kings of the far North. But we were out to be the best in every way. Always a real footballing side, our first-ever FA Cup tie ended in a 5-1 defeat because we were quite literally kicked off the park by a team of Derbyshire miners, several Middlesbrough players were hospitalised. You see we refused to stoop to those lowdown hoodlum tactics, Middlesbrough were above all that.

And we didn't need to, Teesside was so superior in the art of soccer that Middlesbrough and Redcar, yes Redcar met in the 5th Round of the FA Cup. Where were you Arsenal? Where we you Chelsea? Nowhere that's where. I was talking about the strength of Teesside but what about the strength of Middlesbrough itself? In 1888 we were so darned good that we could afford to split into two camps and put out two football teams for the town. Remember that Manchester, think about it Liverpool. We were still a new town, half a century in age, with a tiny population of around 100 000 and yet we had TWO TOP teams, the Nops and the Scabs. Both teams joined the Northern League, Ironopolis turned down the Football League because the opposition wasn't deemed attractive enough. That's the spirit. We don't need those rubbishy league clubs, if you're looking for proper football then look no further than South Bank, Bishop Auckland and Newcastle East and West End's.

Middlesbrough went on to win the Northern League three times in a decade, and bare this in mind Man United. The Northern League is the second oldest league in the whole wide world. How old is the Premier League? Catch my drift? Come back when you've won something with the pedigree of tradition.

If you are still not convinced about our Victorian heyday then how about our successes on the national stage. In 1885 Middlesbrough won an FA Cup, and three years later we won it again. That's the FA Amateur Cup of course, but it's not to be sniffed at. We didn't win another cup until 1976 when it took an own goal to give us a one goal win over two legs to secure the Anglo-Scottish Cup. Wow!

So to sum up let's look at the football balance sheet and what do you see.

20th century - a few 2nd Division Championships, an Anglo-Scotish Cup won against an English second string side, four cup final defeats and a couple of near misses in the top flight. And we've played for the full 100 years.

19th Century - we were only around for 24 years and yet we won three Northern League titles, beat everyone out of sight in the north-east. Had two teams on the go and won two national cup finals.

No contest - so lets go into the new century with renewed hope, put the past hundred years behind us Take a deep breath and say it was just one of those things, a run of bad luck. It's time to look back and take strength from our glorious past. So I'm appealing for a return to the old "lucky" colours of white shirts and blue shorts, it's a bit Spurs I know but we were there first. The old changed strip was black shirts and white shorts, that sounds very Man United. That should go down well with the gaffer. Move over Alex Ferguson. We'll be a changed team next year. Just you wait and see.

The FMTTM Millannual

THEY PLAYED FOR MIDDLESBROUGH

Think back to that misspent youth, when you idled away your time. You should have been doing the same as any normal child of your age and practising wholesome, productive, healthy pursuits like shooting pool or playing pontoon. But oh no that wasn't good enough for you was it? No, you had to be the one burrowing through the pages of Boro reference books testing your little sister on Middlesbrough inside forwards between 1932 to 1938. Don't deny it, because we all know that it's true. Yes, you were that Boro Statto bore.

But looky here swotty Motty for this is one list you won't find in your over-trowelled textbooks. No names and no pack drills from this ripping roll call of fame and fortune will trouble the pages of the esteemed Boro alphabets. For this is the domain of unsung heroes. The Boro players that time forgot, perhaps better known for other achievements, but once upon a time they were Boro through and through.

So now for the first time, in an A4, hard backed, format, Fly Me To The Moon's resident hysterical historian **Gary Hasper** has lifted the veil on the forgotten careers of the men who were proud to hear that Holgate roar.

So without further a do let's go back...back...back to.....

Harold Lloyd

He was signed from California Boys Club, Eston at the turn of the century. It was always going to be either the ironstone mine or the football pitch for young Harry who spent many a carefree hour honing his skills by kicking lumps of pig iron around the pithead. Unfortunately as his parents could not afford to provide him with shoes this meant many an enforced visit to North Ormesby Cottage Hospital to have his broken toes reset. Aye they were hard days but happy all the same for the youngster. But you see how it was with Harold, even as a nipper he liked to push things to the limit, live life on the edge.

Harold Lloyd made his debut as a raw fifteen-year old in a 2 all home draw with Glossop in 1900, the game taking place at the old Linthorpe Road Ground. The young player made an immediate impact with his clever footwork and good movement off the ball. Unfortunately he was rather less well received for cavorting on the floor after a brush with the Glossop defenders. "Stop yer acting and get up off the floor, man" was the cry from an unsympathetic popular end. He also made his mark off the field, a wild night at the Cross Keys was followed by a chase across town from the local cops.

Three years later and it was noted in the North Eastern Daily Gazette that Harold Lloyd had caused a minor sensation at the opening match at Middlesbrough's new home of Ayresome Park. Lloyd was reported to be so incensed with manager John Robson for dropping his name from the team sheet that he scaled the magnificent North Stand in protest, while the game was still in progress. Spectators and players alike could only look on in horror as Lloyd lost his footing on the treacherous barrel-roof. Loud gasps of horror soon turned to cries of unfettered joy as he was saved from certain death by a last gasp grasp for the long hand of the Longines clock (see above).

After the match an enraged Borough Chairman Major Pools lambasted Lloyd in the pages of the North Eastern Daily Gazette, "that young tyke has ruined what otherwise would have been a great and glorious day for the peoples of Middlesborough and Stockton-upon-Tees. He has stolen the thunder and deflected from the glory of the most momentous of occasions as to the opening of a magnificent new sporting facility the like of which has ne'er been seen afore in English Association rules football... Mark my words young Lloyd will never play football again... not so long as I am anything to do with this beautiful game." Manager John Robson was even more scathing when quoted in the Northern Daily Chronicle, Bugle and Echo Journal saying, "Lloyd seems to think he's some sort of acrobat or stuntman. If laughs are what he's after then he's better off in vaudeville with Little Titch. I am washing my hands of the lad now, I want to build this club around quality players, and the only quality he has is for playing the bloody fool."

Harold Lloyd was immediately sent packing and it is often whispered that he took off to the west, taking a fast steamer direct from Jackson's Landing, West Hartlepool to Manhattan. It is thought that Lloyd went on to carve out some kind of a career for himself in the other California. It is even suggested by some celluloid know-it-alls that Lloyd made it big in the land of plenty and shone brightly in Tinsel Town itself. In a recently unearthed archive at the Barry Norman Canned Meat Festival a scratchy black and white short was

The Way They Were

Gordon McQueen

Former Red Devil Gordon McQueen is now a real demon on the oche. Just ask Fabrizio Ravanelli about the gentle giant Scot's double top!

unearthed of a bespectacled Lloyd hanging from the roof of a skyscraper from the hands of a large clock. Perhaps Middlesbrough fans will smell a rat here. And as for the North Stand clock, well it never did work again.

Assisted by Rob Shrug

TEESSIDE TOMMY

NOW THEN FLY ME GADGIES! HEY, FANCY ME GETTING IN THAT OWLD FANZINE EFFORT WITH ROOFUS AND THAT! SMART EH?
Me and Our Tony wrote a letter once about how Kerny was a big spud and that. Never got printed like. Still no hard feelings though, eh?
Here are the votes of the **Streetfighters** jury:

FIVE MATCH VIDEOS

1 Boro 4 Geordies 1 (1990)
Bloody ace eh? We stay up, they stay down, the Wolfman and Yogi stuff the Mags with goals at the Holgate End and Sumo Quinn huffs and puffs all over the shop. One of the finest moments ever at Ayresome Park (RIP).
2 Boro 4 Oxford 1 (1967)
Everyone and his dog lies about how this was their first game and that but I wasn't there coz I was only an ankle-biter then like but me Dad is always waffling on about that John O'Rourke hat-trick. Must be worth a watch eh?
3 Boro 8 Sheff Wed 0 (1974)
Some soft gadgies reckon these games are too one sided and boring to watch... yer joking aren't yer? I remember getting ratted on Double Diamond celebrating and being sick all over me 32 button high waisters outside the Brambles Farm.
4 Boro 7 Chelsea 2 (1978)
If I ever hear some cockney gobbing off about how they always beat us at Wembley and that I just close my eyes and picture Micky Burns banging them four goals in.
5 Boro 3 Newcastle 2 (1983)
I saw the fest two goals but I had to listen to the end on my red plastic tranny in the General after that Heine Otto broke me nose and gave me first degree Bovril burns. I was coming back onto the Holgate with a steaming cup in each hand and a meat pie in me gob when a Heine shot whacked me bang on me bloody hooter like. Snap. It was on telly and everything so I need this one for me personal collection, eh?

MEMORABILIA

Dunno really... I'm not that fussed with all the stuff that sad people collect like. Mind, I wouldn't mind reliving the old matchday experience of the Golden Age of Ayresome Park, recreating the tastes and smells from along the owld route: The Masham, The Shaky, The Alice, The Empire, The Boro Fish Bar, The Westminster. Smart eh?

BORO PERSON

I'm not sure I'd get on with all them modern millionaires like, except Gazza of course coz he sounds a top gadgie. Me all time hero was Mogga but I'm not sure what he's like on the beer. I still reckon Jamie Pollock is top gadgie coz he was sat next to me on one of them big lion efforts in Trafalgar Square the night before Wembley for the Hokey Cokey Cup with Leicester. Minging he was.

The FMTTM Millannual

GEORGE CAMSELL (1930s)
George was one of soccer's all time greats,
Could this be the reason?
345 Boro goals,
59 of them in one season.

The FMTTM Millannual

THEY PLAYED FOR MIDDLESBROUGH

Jacques Cousteau

Boro's own stringy bundle of Gallic charm joined the Middlesbrough team in 1936 to become our first ever foreign import. Unfortunately his impact at the club can be at best described as fleeting. It was sink or swim in those heady days of star names the likes of Mannion, Camsell, Birkett and for young Jacques the competition was to prove all too hot, even hotter than an exploding underwater volcano.

Middlesbrough manager Wilf Gillow was first alerted to the ball playing talents of young Jacques by club director Jack Hatfield. Four times Olympian Jack Hatfield spotted the Frenchman starring in the water polo pool for France in the 1936 Berlin Olympics. He confided to North Eastern Gazette's Boro reporter Captain Jack, "the lad is a natural athlete and possesses a fine pair of lungs." Hatfield watched Cousteau captain his country to the Olympic Final sweeping past the Italians, Japanese and Romanians en route to a head to head with a crack German squad. Hatfield couldn't help be impressed. "He really stuck one up those axis powers," he commented, "and the way he handled himself out there against those Germans, I've rarely seen such spunk in a swimming pool."

High recommendation indeed and Borough manager Wilf Gillow was keen to take a gamble on Cousteau making the transition from the pool to the association football pitch. Could Cousteau be the missing link in the jigsaw Boro had been so desperately seeking? Would Jacques provide the continental flair that could lift the side to that oh so elsuive silverware? Could the Frenchman supply the muscle and hustle to chaperone diminuitive teenage protege Wilfie Mannion to provide the bullets for deadly strike duo Camsell and Fenton? No.

Sadly Jacques Cousteau floundered like a fish out of water. Thrown in at the deep end of a crack English First Division team it proved one step beyond for even our game gallic friend and Jacques was soon setting sail once more. He returned back to his home across the Channel where it is said he eventually found a certain degree of fame and maybe fortune through his invention of the aqualung and pioneering televised underwater explorations of the seven seas. Although alack and indeed alas for poor Jacques, the footballing immortality he so craved at the northern academy of the beautiful game would prove elusive till the end. His last flickering ambition to sit on the esteemed red sofa of Alastair and Bernie would remain sadly unfulfilled. C'est la vie. Comme ce comme ca. Never mind eh!

The Way They Were

Young Stampy puts pen to paper, flanked by dad Stuart and Boro's Ron Bone. "The first thing we'll do Stuart is build the lad up a bit."

Philip Stamp

24

and in a packed programme tonight...
Bob Fischer cuts snippets of genius from the Boro's match programmes of yesteryear

FACE IN THE CROWD
sponsored by J. D. WHITE LTD. (Crane Hire)

1976: THE CELEBRITY-PACKED HOLGATE
Astonishingly ALSO from the Arsenal programme of 28.2.76, an edition that has long since taken on "Holy Grail" status amongst collectors of such gold-dust, the phenomenal "Face in the Crowd" competition. Everybody can spot a magnificent Jarvis Cocker lurking just below the Face in the Crowd himself, but how about also Tucker Jenkins (in front of Jarvis); Malcolm Allison (next but one to Tucker); Lord Lucan (behind the bloke in the checky flat cap); Mike Baldwin (halfway up, second from the right) and Brookside's Bobby Grant (latterly the dad in The Royle Family - behind the Face in the Crowd). Gosh!

MOONSTRUCK
Rob Hymer

Fly: WHAT WAS YOUR FIRST BORO GAME and what kind of things do you remember about it?
Boro versus Sutton United, FA Cup third round replay, 3rd January 1988. I mainly remember:
A/ It was bloody cold, like about ten degrees colder than it was outside Ayresome Park.
B/ It was a bloody awful match (Paul Kerr, who my ex told me was called 'nookie', god knows why, scored in the 110th minute. It was that kind of game).
C/ Even allowing for B/, it was a great experience. Football is dead intense when you see it for the first time as an adult.

Fly: WHAT WAS YOUR BEST EVER BORO MOMENT?
The moment when Alun Armstrong scored the first goal against Oxford on the last day of the 1997-98 season. The mass release of tension was awesome as 30, 000 people went absolutely mental, and the noisy Oxford fans were drowned out by a complete torrent of sound.
Alternatively, my mate Dave and me dancing round a filling station car park near Thirsk like a pair of eejits when Alastair Brownlee announced the final whistle last December 19th. Oddly, we weren't alone.

Fly: WHAT WAS THE LOWEST BORO POINT?
I think it was probably when I first saw Paul Merson in a Villa top last September. The feeling of betrayal that left proved to me what a massive emotional investment supporters make in the game.

THE PALINDROME CASE

Many readers will be familiar with the antics around Teesside in the past few years of that international players' agent, playboy and friend to the stars, Iggi Palindrome whose multinational business empire has its epicentre in a woollens stall at Ormesby market. Over the years Iggy's catchphrase ("All good stuff. No rubbish. C'mon ladies, treat yerselves") has become well known to a legion of Boro's top players including the immortal Fabrizio Ravishankar goal-scorer, sitar-player and good chum of Craig Harrison's dad, George, wayward shaggy-haired Brazilian tup, Emmerdale, and maverick midfield maestro Paul Merton whose hilarious comedic performances have kept audiences in Cleveland chortling for generations.

During his association with players of the top calibre Palindrome has brokered many a deal that has seen his clients leaving from Teesside airport to a soundtrack of cheering fans and club officials yelling "Come back here with our lightbulbs". The story of his most audacious deal, however, has never been told. Until now..........

May 1995

Iggi approaches the Transporter Bridge claiming that he has just received an inquiry about its availability from Milan whose boss Fabio Capello sees "a 225 foot high blue steel structure that only works sporadically" as the natural replacement for the ageing Ruud Gullit. At the same time Palindrome places a story in Italian sports daily Gazetto della Sport that runs next day under the headline "Will No One End My North-East Nightmare? - Want away Industrial Monument's Desperate Plea" and alleges that the Transporter's family have been unable to settle in the area. The next morning Middlesbrough is engulfed in a media storm. A spokesman for the Council says, "The Transporter Bridge is going nowhere".

Star Quality

Milan, meanwhile, deny any approach but also stress that "As a club we are prepared to buy practically anything." A point that is confirmed later in the day when they sign Andreas Andersson.

The Transporter itself seems uncertain about the move, "Middlesbrough has been good to me," it tells the Daily Mirror, "But at the end of the day being a bridge is a short career and I have to think about my long-term future". Asked if it believes it will be able to adjust to life on the continent the Transporter drops another bombshell, "From what I have been told Signor Berlusconi is prepared to pay for ICI Billingham, The Hill Street Centre and a large chunk of Eston to fly over for the first season to stop me getting homesick" he says.

A spokesman for Cleveland Council says, "Believe me when I say Eston is going nowhere," to which many people nod their heads and mutter, "you're telling me".

Meanwhile Palindrome is moving on to the next phase of his plan, phoning Real Madrid to inform them that so far Milan have failed to match the Transporter's personal terms which are believed to include free lubrication and a complete re-paint every two seasons. President Nunez says he is "very interested" in the 2,600 ton bridge.

An hour later Iggy is chatting with Italian sports journalist "I am confident Middlesbrough will let the Transporter go," he says, "After all everybody in England knows that the Newport Bridge is a far greater and more exciting river spanning talent".

The bait is swallowed. That evening the chairman of Lazio sends a fax offering £25million plus Bepe Signori and The Colosseum for "this wonderful 1930s masterpiece with its two powerful 325hp electric motors which lift its central span 120 feet above the water". Iggy says he believes he might be able to interest Middlesbrough in such a deal if Lazio are prepared to take Yarm viaduct as well.

Two days later, after a prolonged media campaign in the region, a candlelit vigil outside the Town Hall and the intervention Mr Tony Blair, the Newport Bridge agrees to stay on Teesside in return for a new improved contract and a loyalty bonus believed to be worth several million. Iggy Palindrome trousers 15% and two minutes later telephones Barcelona with the news that Roseberry Topping is desperate to win some medals.

Harry Pearson

The FMTTM Millannual

The FMTTM Millannual

TONY MOWBRAY

FMTTM - Do you remember your first game for the Boro? (1-1 away at Newcastle, Sept. 1982)

Tony Mowbray - Yes I do remember it, I think Paul Ward was going to make his debut that day as well, I seem to remember my mother's got the cutting of the Evening Gazette back page picture of us leaning over near the dugouts at Ayresome Park. Yes, a baptism of fire but to be honest it happened that quick I didn't really have a chance to worry about it too much. Kevin Keegan was playing for them at the time, it was a night match which added to the atmosphere against Newcastle which added to the intensity of the match. We weren't by a long shot a great side in the early '80s, I was a young lad and I'd worked with Bobby Murdoch as my youth team coach for such a long time and when he got the job he'd obviously seen certain qualities in me and threw me in to what I think was the third game of the season. The game itself...we played a back three, don't remember too much other than the result and the goal we scored, I came up against Keegan a lot but he played a lot of getting the ball to his feet, laying it off and spinning which I was very thankful of. Your worst scenario sometimes, if you get a chance to think about things like that, is that he's going to get it, turn and make you look a fool, but I was thankful for the fact he got the ball, threw a little dummy, laid it off and tried to get in the box. Mick Channon scored and did his famous wheel-away with his arm, Darren Wood scored for us to make it 1-1 and it was a great result for us.

To be honest with you I was never expecting, or knowing as a young footballer, you don't really think I deserve to be in the team, I was never really that arrogant or had such an ego to think that I was better than who was in there and I didn't expect to play. And then after that game I wasn't expecting anything else, I didn't think 'this is me, I'm a first team player I'm going to stay in the team forever'. There was huge relief that the game went quite well on a personal level, first and foremost your career's off, you've played in such a big game. You just remember the euphoria after the game, I was pleased for my family and for the people who were still at the time quite close in your life like school teachers and the sports masters, people like that who were sending you best wishes cards, pleased for them as much as myself that I'd done OK in that game.

FMTTM - Do you remember your last game? (away at Barnsley, Bonfire night 1991, when you waved to the crowd did you know it was for the last time)

TM - Yes I think so, I mean I've got that picture pinned up at home on my wall to be honest in the blue strip with my arm in the air waving goodbye. Very emotional, I knew things were happening, I'd spoke to Lenny about the possibility of moving on, just that year I was finding the motivation side of it hard. Lenny wasn't in the door that long as the manager and I don't think there was fantastic chemistry between us, and I think he knew he had to change personnel at the football club. When any new manager comes in he realises he's got to look around and think what he can change to spark a place up, and maybe he thought I'd been there a long, long time and was a fairly strong influence in the dressing room, maybe he wanted to change that and bring his own people in. There was never any fall outs with Lenny I still bump into him now and I get on great with him, he's a very straight talker which is why I could associate with what he was saying, I like to think that I'm a very straight forward person, there's no hidden agendas with me and he's very much the same. That game, I'd spoke to him during that week and we'd discussed possibly where I could move on to as I was finding the motivational side more difficult at the start of the season. I mean we were doing OK, we were promoted in that season and I think we were second in the league when I left. So it was a big decision but one that I felt I needed a new challenge in my life and in my football career and Celtic came in within a day or so from me first mentioning it to Lenny, asking what price, and it just happened like that, very quickly. I went up to Celtic Park, watched a European game, a fantastic night of football up there and was bitten by the bug.

FMTTM - How did the atmosphere in Glasgow compare to that of the North East in terms of the intensity of the crowds?

TM - The North East's very intense about it's football compared to where I am now, but in Glasgow you've got to multiply that again when you consider the religious aspects of it as well, there's the 'us' and 'them' side of football up there which adds to it a lot. It runs through every facet of life in Scotland, the passion, but at Celtic it's probably even more intense now really because the only success is to win trophies, to win a Scottish Cup, to win the League Cup, to win the League, to beat Rangers, it's only us and them. It doesn't really matter what you get up to against everybody else as long as you're a point above them, you're beating them and then the big games come along and the city goes crazy in the build up to it. I would never say to any player 'don't go to Rangers or Celtic because the league's not the best quality', I know that a lot of people are saying that now. I would take Celtic and Rangers out of that context and think just to play for one of them is a life experience, it's not just playing for a football club, it's a lot more than that. That's probably the best way I can put it, it's always going to be a part of my life that I played for Celtic and I can't pay the club a bigger compliment than to say it touched my heart, the first results I always look for are Middlesbrough and Celtic.

FMTTM - How close were you to rejoining Middlesbrough, when Lenny Lawrence almost re-signed you from Celtic?

TM - It was nearly done, it was virtually done and dusted, I'd even picked a house to be honest. I came down with my girlfriend, soon to be my wife, looked around at the house and sorted out personal terms. Celtic were in financial straits at the time, at the end of the Kelly and Wrights (?) era and although it was quite a paltry

The singing career never quite took off

sum in football terms the deal fell down because ultimately I was the one being asked by Celtic to forego it. Here I was, I wasn't asking for a transfer, Middlesbrough had come in and made an offer and they'd accepted it. General football know how, that's the way the world works in football that if you don't ask for a transfer you get monies owing to you paid up. A matter of principle really, I wasn't going to let myself let them get away with it, really it was a matter of principle. I stayed when they thought I was just going to go back to this club I'd been with for twelve years. It was disappointing for me but at the same time it was fantastic times after that. To be honest I don't look back with regret because of any decision I tend to make in my life, once its made I try and make it positive and just get on with it. I don't know how my life would have gone if I'd gone back to Middlesbgrough at that stage, you'll never know.

FMTTM - What were the high and low points of your time at the Boro?

TM - My career spanned such a long period it encased quite a few highs and lows. Whilst the low points were also the high points at some stages, the liquidation whilst it was a very low point it was a fantastic time to be a player at the club. The affinity that came out of that adversity at the time was special, still is special. I keep in touch with quite a few of those players from that era and am forever looking out for how they're performing, a few of them are back in Middlesbrough obviously! They were great times, at the same time it was a difficult time for the football club, an oxymoron really, a bittersweet period of our careers there, it was a great time.

Disappointing times at Middlesbrough, obviously relegation, I remember laying in the bath flat on my back in the dressing room at Sheffield Wednesday after relegation. Disappointed at missing out at playing at Wembley in the ZDS final, although it wasn't a major final at the time was a huge thing for the club, a huge day out at the time but as it turned out the club have been back a few times since.

Other highlights, every win's a highlight to be honest, I think working with that bunch of players from '86-'88 was a fantastic life experience for me. I just feel so lucky to have had that, maybe that moulded the person that Tony Mowbray was to be. Having worked with Bruce he would still be the first person I would say as the one that moulded my football career. After being washed around in the waves of a club not really knowing where it was going in the early '80s, Bruce gave it some direction and it was great to be a part of that. As a footballer, the highs personally included my debut, which was obviously a big high when you look back at it, and Stamford Bridge which will live with me forever. The aftermath of the game really was fantastic, alright we had to leave the pitch for a bit, but celebrating half an hour after we'd gone off and then to come back out was like a double celebration. The boys, the manager, coaches, the chairman, all the staff in the dressing room straight after the game celebrating. But then to go back on the pitch where there were still hoards of supporters, and being able to celebrate again with them was a great, great time. The season before as well, on top of the directors box after the Wigan game, again was a great night. I still remember Archie's header, everyone coming on the pitch thinking it's in, but off the line, great times. But apart from these incidents because my career spanned so long there it's difficult to pick out any others, as there were so many high points really.

FMTTM - You clearly still look back with fondness on your Boro years with Bruce Rioch?

TM - Yes, I mean Bruce is working down the road at Norwich now, and I'm feeling for him a bit at the moment, probably his four best players have got long term injuries and they're sitting bottom of the league. They've got Darren Eadie out, the boy Mulryne from Manchester United just broke his leg there last weekend, Bellamy who's an international and Matt Jackson, so it doesn't help anybody if they've got four of their top players out. So I feel for him a little bit at the moment, but I know what a good job Bruce can do and he'll get them back on the right road.

FMTTM - How frustrated do you now feel as a coach if players don't seem to be giving their all for the team, as was your trademark style of play at the Boro?

TM - You try and instil your own standards, morals and ideas of play on people but at the same time as a coach you've got to be able to step back and realise that one player's qualities are not going to be another player's qualities. I'd like to think that I can step away from my own playing side, because I was very aware of my own limitations as a player and I knew what I needed to do to overcome my lack of mobility. I had lots of deficiencies in my game but I made sure that they were washed over with all my other qualities that I knew I had. But that was just me as an individual using every resource I had to be the very best player I could be. I try and do that with the players at this football club, get them to look at their own qualities and where they need to strengthen, but whilst you work on people's deficiencies you've got to also make sure you get the maximum out of their strengths. So it's not been a problem for me to think 'we didn't get after the ball enough today', or that 'we didn't have enough commitment', I like to think I'm a little detached from my own personality and think what's most important for our team.

At the moment it's going very well, I've been a coach for seven games and we haven't lost one! Nobody's getting carried away because of the pitfalls along the road, and it's how we react to those bad days and bounce back that's important. But I'm enjoying it immensely at the moment and it's a pleasure to work with such talented players who want to achieve and want to get on. Today's football world is one where there's so much to gain for young players in monetary terms if they're willing to put in the effort and hard work, listen and learn, it's there for them as a golden apple at the end of the road. They've seen the likes of Kieron Dyer leave for £6 million and all the rewards that go with it, the next one could be them if they apply themselves and work. I'm not trying to sell our players but these are all aspects of motivation you can use with players. I'm finding lots of differences on this side of the fence, as a player you don't realise how much goes on, how much thought goes into every decision. As a player you don't see it, you might think, 'well, why has he been picked?' but every decision is thoroughly thought through. One of the biggest differences is the hours you put in, as a player I was on the settee at half past one most afternoons in the week, now I'm not getting home until five or six o'clock because of preparation for the next day, discussing what you did today, discussing how you're going to play at the weekend, discussing the opposition, where we've got to watch games and players. It's hard work but it's what I love and it still doesn't seem like work to me.

FMTTM - As you know 'Fly Me To The Moon' was in some way named after you, as it would have been you that Bruce Rioch would have taken with him on such a journey, who would you take with you on a trip into space?

TM - To be honest I think that's a difficult question, at the time the context of that question I think we'd just played Everton in a Cup replay and I'd scored a last minute equaliser taking it to extra time. I think that the reporter asked Bruce on Midweek Sports Special or whatever it was, 'What about this guy Tony Mowbray', and that was the analogy that he used that if he was to fly to the moon the one person he'd want next to him was me and obviously that stuck. As a player I wouldn't want to say that somebody was better than someone else. If I become a manager and one of my players is showing the spirit that's taking the team along, then possibly I might say something. But I wouldn't like to... I mean there's lots, especially at this football club at the moment, lots of players who are playing football for the right reasons, want to be successful and want to take Ipswich into the Premiership, so all those players really.

and in a packed programme tonight...
Bob Fischer cuts snippets of genius from the Boro's match programmes of yesteryear

1990: PLAYERS AT HOME WITH THEIR PARENTS

For a short time in the early nineties, it wasn't enough for the programme to include fantastic action shots of our heroes in action, eg Bernie Slaven (out of shot) passes to Gary Hamilton (obscured by post) who shoots past Tony Coton (on ground) while Archie Stephens (behind photographer) celebrates.

No, for some unnatural reason the weekly Player Profile had to include a passport sized photo of our victims with either a) a bouffanted and eye-shadowed wife/girlfriend or b) for the young lads (or the suspected homosexuals), their parents. Two classic examples feature here. Firstly, we see Nicky Mohan "relaxing" underneath the arches (girlfriend Nicola Wade, "a local hospital receptionist from Linthorpe" not pictured) and then future Darlington star Michael "Rodney" Trotter at home with his parents Barry Chuckle and Dora Bryan.. And you thought your family portraits were bad. Phooey.

 **MOONSTRUCK**

1. FIRST BORO GAME ATTENDED? I can't remember the first full game I saw, but I certainly remember the first time I went to Ayresome Park, even though I was only seven years old. Because we lived close to the ground, my brother Pete taught me how to see the Boro for nowt, even if it was for only twenty minutes, and that was to wait outside the ground until they opened the gates (yes, those damn early leavers, "missing the rush"). As I walked up the steps, I became aware of the lights, then the shock of seeing a vast stadium in front of my young eyes and that bright, bright green grass. The red shirts popping around chasing the blur of white. They were playing Brighton. Life had changed.

2. BEST TIME TO EVER BE A BORO FAN? Our first real appearance at Wembley in the Coca Cola Cup final, that period of time just after that grey haired bloke, who had scored the winning goal in the previous season's European Cup Final, put Boro one nil up against Leicester. Hairs rise on the back of my neck just thinking about it.

3. WORST? About twenty minutes later. Leicester's equaliser. We all bit back the feeling of "Hey, we're going to win this!" because we knew that Boro always had the ability to kick you in the teeth when you had dropped your guard and became all optimistic. At the final whistle, you'd have thought we had lost. And of course we had. I've lain awake at night since, just piecing together what would have happened if Emile Heskey had not put that ball over the line. Just think about that...

The FMTTM Millannual

when the mud sticks

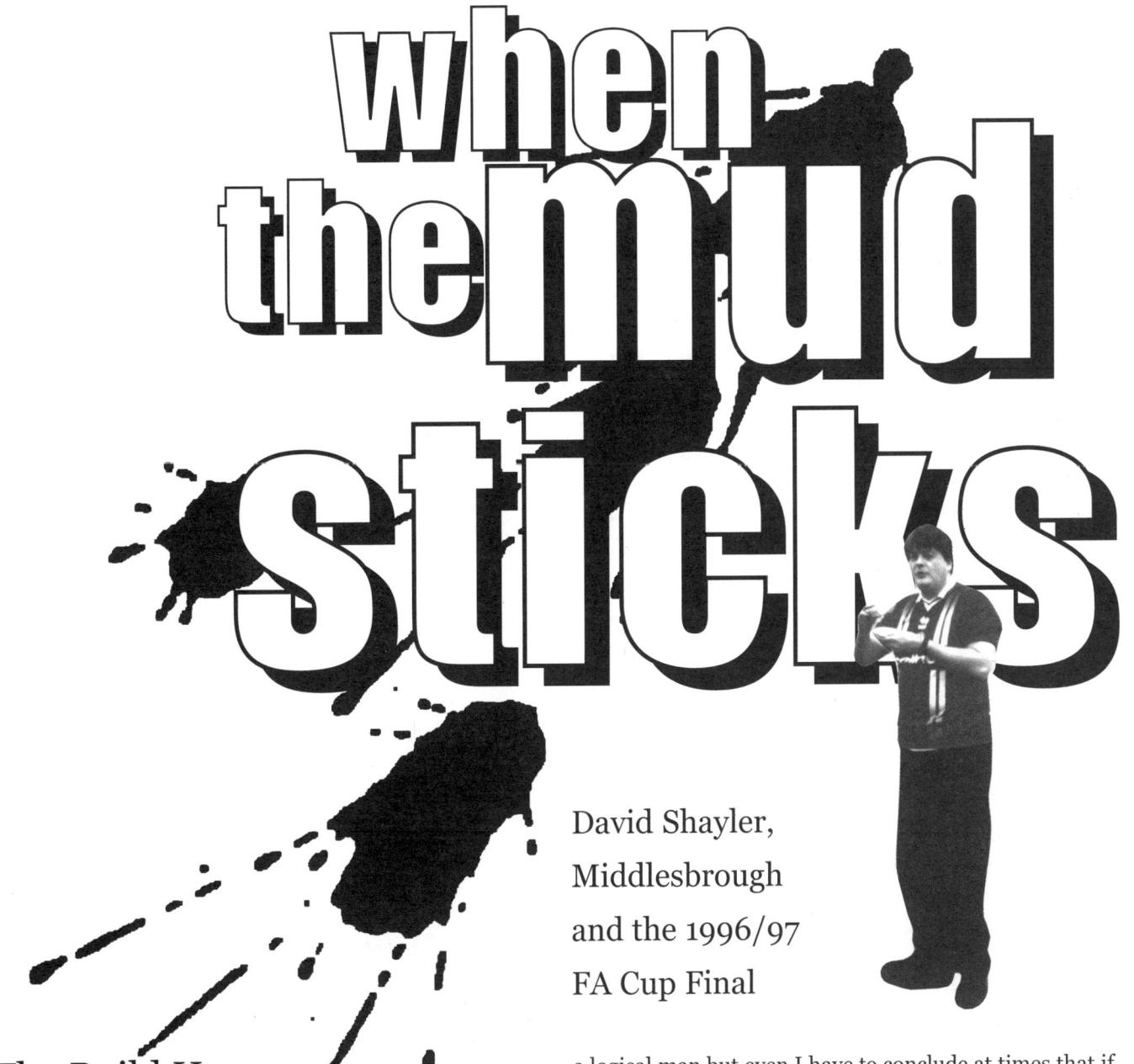

David Shayler, Middlesbrough and the 1996/97 FA Cup Final

The Build Up

Middlesbrough were relegated on Sunday 11 May 1997 after a 1-1 draw away at Leeds, when a win would have secured a place in the Premier League for the 1997/98 season. I could barely get up come the Monday morning. Why us? Why did we have to be the team who got relegated because the Premier League gave us bad advice one Friday in December and then had the temerity to punish us for it. Why did we get relegated by exactly the three points we were deducted as a result? To make matters worse, Coventry who once again looked dead and buried beat Spurs to stay up. Everyone hates Coventry and they would have gone down if we had not had our three points stolen. They are a dour side who play the game without flair, have no history, no backing and yet every season have lucky breaks which help them stay up despite overwhelming odds.

Some teams, like some people, seem to have all the luck. And sometimes you cannot escape this glaring fact. I am a logical man but even I have to conclude at times that if luck is not on your side, as it seldom is in Middlesbrough's case, you are condemned to a life of misery. Football fans elsewhere were not going to stand up for us, despite us playing some of the most attractive football in the country. We were northern upstarts who should know our place, or so the London media claimed. I spent the week in the build up to the Cup Final fervently hoping that the courts would save us from the slow death of Division One. How I believed then in the rule of law. I couldn't even think about the Cup Final. And I tried, believe me I tried. I even bought Trevor Brooking's guide to the Final. Middlesbrough's recent fame (or is it notoriety?) has left me immune to seeing them plastered across the covers of the increasingly abundant, and proportionately lower quality, football glossies which now adorn the shelves of our newsagents in the same way that women's magazines do. Or perhaps I really was just getting older, getting less committed to the cause. The FA Cup Final? I can't be arsed.

31

But on the way home from work on the Friday evening, it began to sink in: Middlesbrough were to play in their first FA Cup Final, in a competition which was founded only four years before the Boro but on which the Boro had left so little impression. I imagined Big Nige walking up the Wembley steps and lifting the cup and us all shouting, cheering, screaming like teenage girls at a Take That concert. I searched for comparisons in my life which might help me prepare for this historic moment: falling in love; my first kiss; my first shag.

None of them, I imagined, would adequately equate in my mind to the climax I thought might be mine, the climax to an agonisingly slow 22 year wait where I had experienced excitement in broad terms but had never really come close to climaxing. No, that is the wrong image: it suggests too much control, too much impetus driven by me when in fact I was trussed up and teased by a virginal teenage temptress. She knew how to give enough to keep me interested all right yet never dreamed of letting me go all the way. But that Friday, my toes were peddling and my muscles were clenching for the first time in my supporting life. It is such a pity it turned out to be premature expectation.

Pre-Match Warm Up

I woke up at midday, cursing myself for missing the first three quarters of an hour of the build up on Grandstand. I tried so hard to get my head around it all. I remembered the Cup Final Grandstands as a child and all that went with it:

· Cup Final It's a Knockout refereed by Arthur Ellis, the man who denied Middlesbrough a semi-final place in 1947 with two diabolical refereeing decisions (although I only learnt that he was the referee responsible in an article earlier that week in The Guardian by Harry Pearson, Boro fan to the literati).

· Cup Final Mastermind and how I vowed that I would be on it and would win it, even at the age of 11, if Middlesbrough ever went to an FA Cup Final.

· The build up to each final on the BBC which seemed to take forever and was punctuated by the odd diversion to ITV, just to see what was happening there.

· Then the finals themselves and particularly the classics:
  · Southampton beating Man U 1-0 in 1976;
  · Arsenal nearly throwing it away in 1979 but scoring again in the last minute to win it;
  · Man U 3 Crystal Palace 3 in 1990, my first final after enduring the long dark winter of Scottish football while at college in Dundee.

Phil and Jem, my brothers, were supposed to come round for midday to share the build up before we went to the match together. I wasn't that bothered they were late but, and this was a galactic but, they had my ticket for the game. By half twelve I had phoned up both their flats but there was no reply from either. They were obviously on the way, I reasoned, as I tried to savour the day despite the nagging worry. I watched Des Lynam interview Steve Gibson, our chairman whose baby-faced enthusiasm for the Boro single-handedly destroyed the image of the bloated plutocrat football chairman. He shared our anger, our outrage, our sense of injustice over the three points deducted.

I watched as the Boro throng came together from the M1 and Kings Cross as one great tidal wave of red and white engulfing West London. On TV, Geoff Vickers, the secretary of the Middlesbrough Supporters Club South, echoed all our sentiments when he described the victory against Derby in the quarter final as the greatest day in the history of the club, especially as he had been to the four quarter final defeats from 1975 to 1981. I felt the tribalism again: the belonging, the shared aims, the fraternity of it all.

But I was also getting increasingly distracted as the clock ticked towards one o'clock and there was still no sign of Phil and Jem. I phoned them both three, maybe four times but there was no reply. I began to think the worst. What if they've crashed? With my Cup Final ticket. I started to calculate how long it would take for me to trace the journey between my flat in Pimlico and Phil's place in Clapham. But what if I found their crashed car? Jesus, how unseemly would it look to the inevitable pedestrian rubberneckers as I frantically piled into the wreckage of bloodied limbs and contorted metal to pluck my Cup Final ticket from the mangled pocket of a dying man:

- They would have wanted it this way, I would have shouted in triumphant justification to the gathered onlookers.
And Phil and Jem would have. I know I certainly would.

On the Road

They finally arrived at about one thirty - an easy trip from SW1 to Wembley you might think. But it wasn't to be that easy. Phil had to go to the wedding reception for Gav, one of his oldest friends, in Buckinghamshire after the game so we had to drive to Hillingdon first, leave the car there and get the Metropolitan line to Wembley Park. The build up to the wedding was a comic tale in itself. When the fixture list had come out, Phil had mentioned in passing that Gav, a friend who didn't like football, was getting married on Cup Final day. And as we all say in these situations in jest but with a tinge of hope:
- Wouldn't it be funny if...
But this time it happened. It actually happened. Part of the comedy was the gradual way it insinuated itself into Phil's life. At first it was a joke.
Then before we knew it we were in the quarter final. Phil resolved not to broach the subject with Gav until the last possible moment as, knowing the Boro, they could fluff it at any stage. On the evening we beat Derby County in the quarters, Phil went out with Gav and some other mates. One of the mates let on that we were in the semis and that the final was the same day as Gav's wedding.
- You'll have to miss it, Gav had said.
- Yeah, Phil agreed but not making it clear what exactly the 'it' referred to in this case.
After the first draw against Chesterfield in the semis, Phil phoned up Gav. Men only phone each other if it is absolutely necessary, and then only to impart hard concrete information. Phil phoned Gav and spoke to him at length. Then he had to deliver the denoument:
- Er, I can't come to your actual wedding 'cos I'm going to the FA Cup Final, he bravely explained, adding by way of consolation, - but I can make the reception afterwards.
In the end Gav hadn't been surprised - the girly-chat length of the conversation had given away Phil's motives but Gav was still pretty miffed that one of his best friends wasn't going to be at this wedding. But, hell, we'd all do the same in Phil's case. If it had been me, I would probably have cowarded out of the reception as well after our abysmal performance.

- I told him, diplomatically of course, that there was far more chance of him being married again than Boro getting to another FA Cup Final, Phil explained to ease his conscience on the way to Wembley that day.
- It's probably more likely that Gav will get divorced and re-marry the same woman than Boro getting to another FA Cup Final, I joked.
- Anyway, we're not as close as we used to be and, if we lose, it's gonna be bad enough at the reception.
- Don't even think about it.
And that was really the only mental preparation we had all made for defeat: Just don't think about it.

Pre-Match Nerves

As usual, the weather for Cup Final day was magnificent. There seems to be a special spell woven over North West London which decrees that it cannot be anything other than brilliant sunshine from 2 pm on Cup Final day. As a kid, it might rain in Beaconsfield, only 15-20 miles down the road, but Wembley would be filled with sharp

shadows cast by the bright sun. On our Cup Final day, we left an overcast, drizzly Pimlico at one thirty but arrived to a scorching Wembley Way an hour later. I wasn't hungry after the night before but I knew I had to eat. I was also very dehydrated. I bought some overpriced junk food from one of the vans on Wembley Way, which was easy as it was deserted by this time. Unlike the Coca Cola Final, we didn't experience the stream of red and white flooding to Mecca. And this time, onimously, Wembley was bedecked in blue and white, the colours of Littlewoods rather than the red and white of Coca Cola earlier in the season. Still, we joked, that red and white omen had done sod all good. Phil bought us all programmes even though, in our crazed superstitious consciousness, we fervently believed this would be bad luck but we had to have the mementoes of the day.

We finally made it into the ground around quarter to three. The emotion of the day, my late night and the lack of food absorbed by my system brought me to a complete standstill as we walked around the curve to our seats. My head span and for a second I really thought I wasn't going to make it. Torrents of sweat poured from my hot, swollen head and my burning armpits, as I stood there trying to drink in the occasion. But I was in reality about to faint. Even if I made it up the steps, I began to think it was evens that I would last the match. Calling on all my reserves, I forced myself up to the second tier. As I climbed the steep steps, the emotional strains of 'Abide with Me' drifted down the stairwell. I stopped and felt my throat swell and my eyes well up. This was it: we were here. We had done it. I stepped into daylight and an inferno of sound and emotion.

We sang and we cheered. We all got behind them. Together, we booed the FA for a good ten minutes for relegating us. When Saturday Comes later commented that they thought we were booing the royals and Buck House would be ablaze by the evening. If only. Or how about Lancaster Gate? And then - high on all this intense outpour of anger, joy and betrayal - as one the 25,000 Middlesbrough fans rose for an emotional moment that I will never forget as long as I am a sentient human being. It began as a haunting melody, like a whisper drifting across the dusty stands into the enticing green playing area below, but was quickly taken up by everyone. Every Boro fan there that day filled their lungs to roar our song. And it is our song alone. Not 'You'll never walk...'; not some shared and therefore diluted campfire ditty; not some other generic totem. But the song we have made our own within football after borrowing it from the American civil rights movement. It was sung by the Boro faithful in the 60s when the long dark days of the old 2nd division seemed like they would never end and has been restored from time to time in moments of unity, like the last game at Ayresome Park. Then, the words were whispered uncertainly like the hollow, chill wind blowing across the industrial badlands of Teesside. This time, it surged from the faithful with pride, with belonging, with the kind of full heartedness required to overcome faltering voices, cracked with the long overdue release of pent-up emotion:

- *We shall overcome. We shall overcome. We shall overcome. Some Day.*

- *Oh, deep in my heart, I do believe, we shall overcome some day.*

- *Oh, deep in my heart, I do believe, we shall overcome some day.*

And each time, hoarse, dry throats seemed to be about to give it up, re-emerging voices took hold of it, breathing new life into it.

By the end, my vocal chords had collapsed and only every second or third syllable escaped into the Wembley auditorium. Tears streamed down my face, as sweat had done earlier, and as the ghostly echo of the final 'Some day, my friend...' wafted across the converted terraces, I caught the eye of some tattooed Teesside hard nut who was also openly sobbing:

- Bluddy ell, it alwiz gets uss that song, he declared cheerfully as he wiped the tears from his eyes.

Seconds later we were cheering as the match kicked off. Seconds after that we were 1-0 down.

The One Minute Final

All I can remember now is stunned disbelief. And seeing the Chelsea fans going mental. Something about the atmosphere - and no doubt the pollution which hangs over London - gave the whole scene a hazy surreal air to it, like a field filled with gunsmoke after a battle.

- We wait 121 years for our first FA Cup Final and we can only enjoy it for 43 seconds, I thought, - this just about sums up our season. It just about sums up the history of the club.

The Boro fans looked at each other in bemusement. Yes, the ball had crept between our keeper Ben Roberts and the bar. Yes, it was nestling in the back of the net. I went into denial. Couldn't they disallow it? You're not allowed to score this early on the Cup Final. I tried to dredge up an early goal from my FA Cup Final conscious but the best I could come up with was ten minutes, West Ham v Arsenal 1980. Many fans still refer to the 1979 final when Arsenal beat Man Utd 3-2 as the 'Five Minute Final' as, if it had finished after 85 minutes, it would have been an instantly forgettable 2-0 victory for Arsenal. Looking back, even after two minutes, I was convinced that I was part of what would become the 'One Minute Final' as that is how long the match lasted as a competitive concept. And it got worse. After twenty minutes, Rav - a risk from the beginning - was injured in a clash with the keeper. Less than half an hour gone and Robbie Mustoe, my player of the season after of course Juninho, realised he couldn't run off a knock and was pulled off. And that was really it. Of course, it's never over until the fat man in black blows the whistle so we all lived in blind hope that somehow we could salvage something from this. But we never really got going.

The crowd-team relationship is a dynamic. In theory, it somehow starts when either the team do something good on the pitch and in response the crowd get behind the team or when the crowd get in full voice and the team rise to the encouragement. In practice, it is not entirely clear what prompts it. And it is a precarious dynamic: it can easily be a vicious rather than a virtuous circle. In the 1997 FA Cup Final, we never really had anything to get excited about. So we were lacklustre and so were the players.

There is one moment that haunts us though. Gian Luca

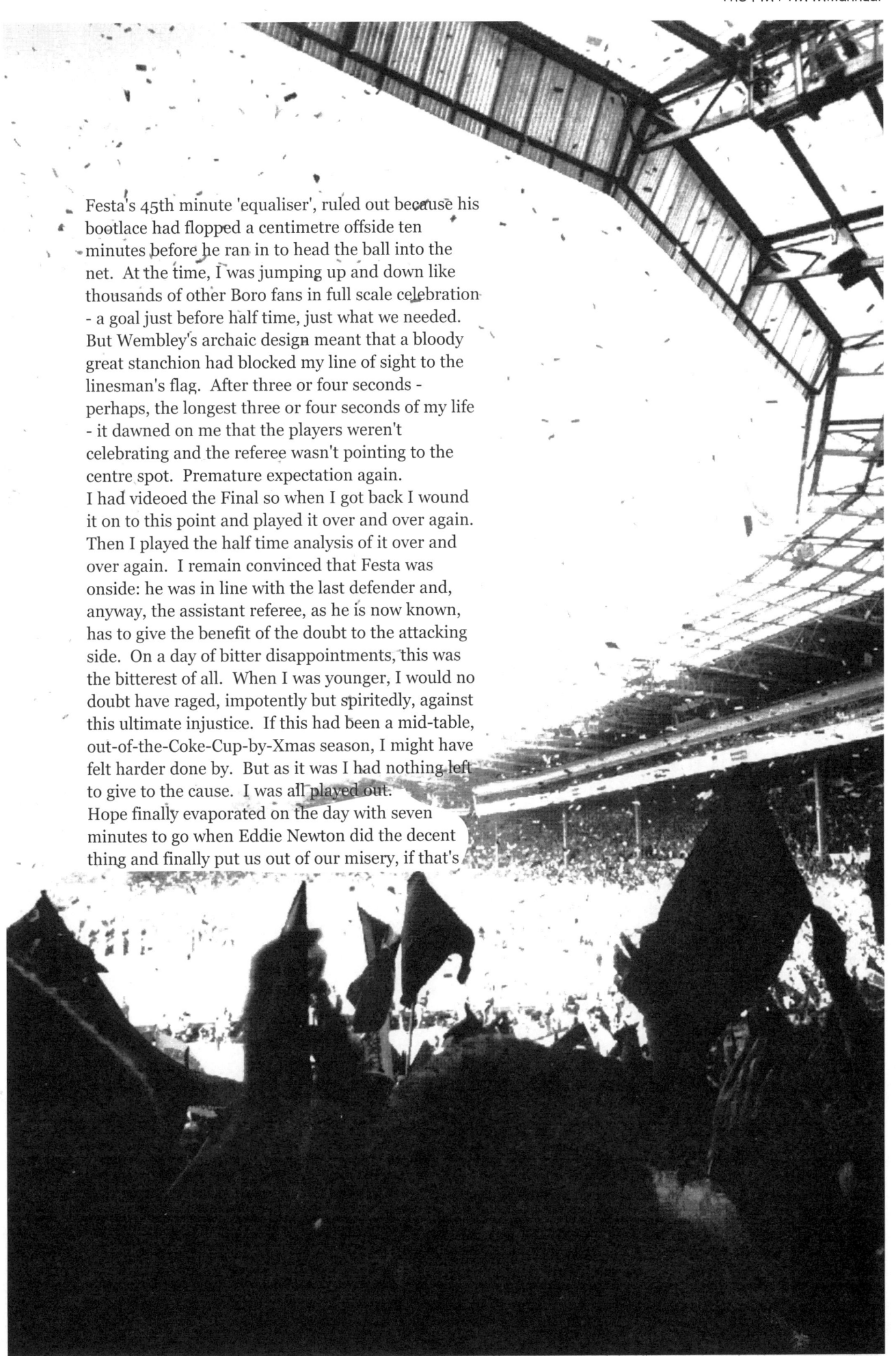

Festa's 45th minute 'equaliser', ruled out because his bootlace had flopped a centimetre offside ten minutes before he ran in to head the ball into the net. At the time, I was jumping up and down like thousands of other Boro fans in full scale celebration - a goal just before half time, just what we needed. But Wembley's archaic design meant that a bloody great stanchion had blocked my line of sight to the linesman's flag. After three or four seconds - perhaps, the longest three or four seconds of my life - it dawned on me that the players weren't celebrating and the referee wasn't pointing to the centre spot. Premature expectation again.

I had videoed the Final so when I got back I wound it on to this point and played it over and over again. Then I played the half time analysis of it over and over again. I remain convinced that Festa was onside: he was in line with the last defender and, anyway, the assistant referee, as he is now known, has to give the benefit of the doubt to the attacking side. On a day of bitter disappointments, this was the bitterest of all. When I was younger, I would no doubt have raged, impotently but spiritedly, against this ultimate injustice. If this had been a mid-table, out-of-the-Coke-Cup-by-Xmas season, I might have felt harder done by. But as it was I had nothing left to give to the cause. I was all played out.

Hope finally evaporated on the day with seven minutes to go when Eddie Newton did the decent thing and finally put us out of our misery, if that's the right phrase. Many of the faithful with their hardened Teesside cynicism got up and started to file out. Minutes later, the final whistle went and Phil shot off to Gav's wedding reception. But me and Jem stayed. We watched the chosen ones wearily climb the Wembley steps, the long day's work done but not complete. They walked towards us and the tunnel, disappointed and broken men, trying to wave, trying to display some final resilience. I watched Juninho, a metaphorical giant among men, disappear into the tunnel, knowing that this was inevitably his last time in a Boro shirt.

I felt numb, I felt strangely unemotional, I felt dislocated. I realised only then that the FA Cup is only about winners. Grandstand shows endless coverage of them interspersed with brief, fleeting shots of the losers which was why this Cup Final was so different. I looked up longingly as I saw Dennis Wise pick up the trophy and turn his back on us to an explosion of flashguns through the London smog. I tried to imagine what it would have been like if it had been us not them. But it was beyond me. And I live in fear that I will never experience the natural high of victory in a major competition.

Perhaps I knew deep down in my heart when we sang 'Two cups and we're staying up' all those months ago, we really should have been singing 'No cups and we're going down'. After all that would be the realistic expectation of the seasoned Boro fan. That's the kind of treble we do. But for that day - and I didn't really appreciate it at the time - we were up there with the best of them.

Post Cup Final Blues

I struggled into work on the Monday but by the Wednesday I had gone down with the flu. I can't be sure whether it was due to the bug that was going around or the football-induced depression but I took the rest of the week off. During this time, both my brothers phoned. It was like mourning the death of a close relative: we were consoling each other, making sure that we weren't going to do anything stupid in response to this final part of the calamity, the final act in a three part tragi-farce. Three months before the Final, my grandmother had died in Middlesbrough where she had lived all her life. I did not even attend the funeral and, to be honest, those who went did so out of duty, rather than from any sense of deep mourning or loss. But me and my brothers consoling each other after the Cup Final was the genuine and deeply felt emotion of a family united in grief.

Yet we could not even mourn properly. Middlesbrough's Premier League existence lay there in a coma in front of us: not yet finally consigned to the afterlife of Division One but its chances of survival slim and against the odds.

- I cannot even begin to assess now the long term effect that goal two minutes from time in the Coca Cola Cup final might have on the club, I confided to Phil desperately. - Remember Notts County voted on the formation of the first Premier League in 1992. But they never played in it and are now in League Division Three. I can't face that. I would rather we went bankrupt. At least then, we could all get on with our lives.

I said that I really did, still hoping that as a result of legal action, we would be given back our rightful place in the Premier League.

- You don't really want that, said Phil disbelieving.
- Oh but I do, I really do. Despair I can live with, hope I cannot.

If say, Man Utd or Liverpool or Everton had beaten us, I could have lived with occasional glimpses on the telly of the victor's inevitable homecoming parade. But it was Chelsea. So the whole process of coming to terms with defeat was, of course, made more difficult by our circumstances, particularly mine. I live in SW1 about two miles from Stamford Bridge. Chelsea are my de facto "local team". And the fickle desire to be associated with victory was demonstrated everywhere by the terminally shallow and those aiming to make a fast buck. Local shopkeepers and publicans - suddenly claiming lifelong fealty to Chelsea - sought to demonstrate this by displaying tacky posters of the team with the FA Cup. Local TV carried features for days. The local press, including the appalling freebies shoved through our door, also capitalised on this success, writing endless stories about how Chelsea's long threatened resurgence had finally come to pass.

To tell you the truth, I couldn't even get angry with them. A younger me might have blamed Chelsea in some way (I've held a grudge against QPR since the 1970s for fooling referees into awarding a series of dodgy penalties against us, usually caused by their players hurling themselves to the floor in the box). But they were the better team on the day. My feelings probably most closely approximated to jealousy: why weren't we the ones with the posters all over town?

As the weeks went by, we waited for Gibson our chairman to make his plan known regarding an appeal against our relegation: how far would he push the football authorities? In this new age of big-business-football, how much influence could he wield? How seriously would the courts take a claim against the FA? And on what grounds? After all, one day, a club which was a Plc might find itself in the same position as the Boro - relegated by virtue of the decree of a bunch of unaccountable idiots in suits rather than as a result of anything on the field. Then, how would the shareholders, Parliament and the courts react?

With football a big business, we cannot let the amateurs and blunderers who currently run the game in this country continue to make these basic mistakes. I am glad we booed the FA officials at their cup final. After all, the FA Cup final is too full of dreadful middle class worthies from the county FAs. Football is still the people's game so at least we had a chance to make ourselves heard. I have thought seriously about going around to Graham Kelly's house and doing him over - not too badly but it would be hard to see how I could ruin his life as much as he has ruined mine - and I am not a violent man.

As time went on, and in the absence of any public announcement from the chairman, cruel rumours started to circulate. One friend said he would be very worried if he were a Coventry fan; another spoke of Sky insisting on a 21 team Premier League to avoid the season being held up pending legal action. I never let my hopes be built up too high. I knew that UEFA would not allow a club to take its governing body to court. But it was tempting, too tempting to believe anything...

Epilogue

On Monday 26 May 1997, the day of the 1st division play off final, now the traditional last day of the English season, my partner Annie and I decided to go and see a film. As we walked to Victoria Station to get a bus up West, we were surrounded by Palace fans behaving boisterously as football fans do.

- I can't get way from it, said Annie in the slightly petulant tone she adopts for football.

Before that match started we decided on the spot to see Fever Pitch, the adaptation of the Hornby meisterwerk. For once with a film the timing was right. As Henderson scored for Palace I was watching Michael Thomas scoring the most famous goal in football history. You know the one. Every football fan does. Every football fan who doesn't support Arsenal tries to imagine just what that would have been like to win the title in the last minute of the season, as Arsenal did in 1988/89 against Liverpool. And remember, until that moment, Liverpool were going to make history. They were about to become the first English club to win the double twice. Paul, the fictitious hero of Fever Pitch the film, reflects that supporting Arsenal would never be the same again once he'd been through his Michael Thomas moment. Annie said indignantly:

- You've never had that moment so you'll never give up football. Will you?

- Perhaps I am still waiting for my Michael Thomas moment. Unfortunately with the Boro it may never come.

- I don't think I can take this any more, she sighed, resigned.

But she will.

And anyway what does she mean she can't take it anymore?

But perhaps she's right. Perhaps I'll never have that moment. But Jesus, we came pretty close in the 1996/97 season. There have been times as a Boro fan that I've thought we might never go to Wembley (in a major competition) or go to an FA Cup semi-final, let alone final. But at least I sat in that crowd at Wembley on 17 May 1997, even if the dream only lived for 43 seconds. I want to cry just remembering it, as I did at the time. So, all together now:

We shall overco-ome. We shall overco-ome. We shall overcome some day-ay-ayyy...

London, July 1997

While Viv was getting ready for a big match he accidentally pulled the knob off his locker door. He then played his best ever game, actually scoring a hat-trick. From that day on he kept the knob as his lucky charm... it never leaves his side.

They Played for Middlesbrough

Neville Chamberlain

Although Neville Chamberlain was never actually to play in the Football League for Middlesbrough he followed up a season of wartime appearances with almost twenty years of active service behind the scenes for his hometown club.

It was after this that Chamberlain then made his move into the national and indeed international political arena for which he is perhaps better remembered today. However, his former parliamentary ally Anthony Eden later recalled in his memoirs that Chamberlain made the surprising admission of having learned many important lessons whilst serving Middlesbrough FC. "Dealing with Herr Hitler and Signori Mussolini was childs-play when compared to negotiating with the ivory towers of the Football Association and those working class inbreeds at the Football League." It seems even the betrayal and humiliation of appeasement paled in comparison to a clash with the football authorities, which was to blight his Middlesbrough career.

It was the height of the depression and unemployment was rife on Middlesbrough. The public could hardly afford to eat properly never mind pay the admission cost at Ayresome Park. As club secretary it was up to Chamberlain to keep the club afloat on a day to day basis and it needed all his skills as a diplomat to balance the books. Although the rates were always well in arrears he managed to win over the council by letting out the changing rooms as a soup kitchen, the team bath was put to use as a giant cauldron to heat up the prize pea and ham and oxtail. Unfortunately there were sometimes complaints of the soup having a head on it and trainer Charlie Cole was instructed to cut the team's coal tar into the merest of slithers to prevent any soapy soup repeating on the hungry diners.

Sadly gate receipts dropped off alarmingly; Chamberlain instigated an immediate investigation the results of which made alarming reading. It was discovered that owing to malnutrition at least half of the crowd was able to get a "squeeze" through the turnstiles. A further quarter or so were able to pass their legs right around the barriers on account of their rickets. So it was a real struggle to match the minimum wage demands of the squad, which at this time was set "at the exorbitant rate" (Borough Chairman Jeremiah Warrenby JP) of half a crown a month. Neville Chamberlain solved this taxing problem by leasing out the players for afternoon work at Lowcocks farm, "gasing up the pop." Thus by clever negotiation, sometimes almost bordering on brinkmanship Chamberlain managed to keep the club afloat.

But still they were dark times for Middlesbrough FC, with little to break the daily drudge. Then in the springtime of 1931 Chamberlain received an official Football League package in his postbag. Inside were twenty tickets for the English showpiece the FA Cup Final at the Empire Stadium, Wembley. Chamberlain was delighted by the news; he now had a most welcome inducement to inspire the players. After the Chairman Sir Jeremiah Warrenby had taken his rightful entitlement the playing squad had two seat tickets left to enjoy...

But as the big day approached the newspapers were filled with shock news of most dastardly events. The FA had uncovered evidence of a massive cup final forgery scam centred somewhere in the, and I quote, "those dirty mills and hills of the northern outposts of our glorious Empire, still a hotbed of lawless dissent and outlawry." Chamberlain was stung into action phoning first the Football League headquarters at Lytham St Annes and then the Football Association itself at Lancaster Gate. He sought immediate confirmation of the validity of the tickets but was less than totally reassured by the League's ill-considered approach. "'Appen they're oil reet, 'appen they're not. Ow can we tell you owt unless we sees em face to face like, our kid." The Football Association refused to respond to the phone call, Chairman Lord Arthur Gall only recognising the telegraph as an acceptable means of communication.

Chamberlain now brokered an extraordinary meeting between himself; the Football League and the Football Association on the neutral ground of Herbert Chapman's canal barge on the Aire and Caulder Navigation at Ferrybridge. After over an hour of intensive negotiation Chamberlain suddenly reappeared on the towpath holding the tickets aloft victoriously. He then made an announced to the waiting media scrum "In my hand I have a piece of paper....." It was a historic moment; the FA and Football League had ratified the cup final tickets. Middlesbrough could now go forward and get on with the season.

But as the weeks went by there were further reports casting a shadow of doubt over the ticket's validity. On the very eve of the Wembley final itself there were noises from both Lord Arthur Gall and the Football League's Arthur Hardwater apparently rubbishing the Middlesbrough tickets. Again Chamberlain lost no time in taking action. He spoke through the mouthpiece of the gentlemen of the press, "I have asked for a further undertaking that these tickets are genuine..... I want to hear by 11o'clock or I will be forced to conclude that the tickets are not bone fide." The 11am deadline came and passed with no word from the authorities, Chamberlain had no choice but to go to his players, "It is with great regret that I have to announce that the cup final tickets are not genuine."

Chamberlain had been duped; Middlesbrough had been caught on their uppers. The secretary's whole demeanour was cast in the shadows. Shortly afterwards he resigned and quietly slipped out of football forever. The rest as they say is history.

R. Shrug

The FMTTM Millannual

GEORGE HARDWICK (1940s)
Georgie Hardwick played full back,
He had a great left foot,
A captain to lead, a turn of speed
And a gentleman to boot.

The FMTTM Millannual

THE SECRET DIARY OF CRAIG SUMMERDALE AGED 20 AND A QUARTER

THURSDAY 14TH OCTOBER 1999

I was walking around the Riverside Stadium today trying to steer clear of Mr Festa (he says I have to give him half my dinner money every day or he'll have the Mafia put a donkey's head in my bed. Attached to a donkey's body. That's right, I'll have to spend the night with Neil Redfearn) when I heard agitated voices.

"Lower!" Mr Robson was groaning from inside his office. "Lower.... LOWER!!!" At first I thought Mr Mustoe must be on back-scratching duties with the ceremonial wooden claw but then the door burst open and a very familiar figure emerged looking rather shaken. Those piercing eyes, those sunken, be-stubbled cheeks and an arse familiar to half of Teesside - that's right, I'd recognise Gabby Yorath anywhere. Only joking of course dear diary, it was that nice Mr Slaven from the radio, Millennium Radio I think it's called and he works there with a man called Mr Brownlegs. Mummy says I have to keep away from Mr Brownlegs because he has mad, stary eyes and he's easily excited. Anyway there was obviously some sort of argument going on.

"Ah'm only bein' honest, that's mah job, y'knoo" Mr Slaven was saying. "If I didnae say what ah think what kinda furtball pundit would ah be?"

"I still can't believe you think we'll finish LOWER than last season" fumed Mr Robson. "Now get out, and while you're at it stop talking in that RIDICULOUS accent! You're not on the radio now you know, you can use your REAL voice with me."

"Terribly sorry, old sauce" said Mr Slaven in clipped Queen's English. "Anyway must dash, Curly's on Jankers and I'll be late for the Gymkhana! Pip Pip!" and with that he raced off in a hurry, so fast in fact that I had to hide behind Mr Robson's gold statue of Clayton Blackmore (he insists that everyone passing the office salutes it every day) just to avoid being seen. It did give me something of an idea, though. Perhaps my ambition to make it into the first team could be fulfilled if I could raise my media profile! With that I made it my sincere vow to get myself on the radio...

My plan, dear diary, was a simple one. Thanks to a daring combination of cunning, instinct and a small bucket of make-up from that little shop in the Forbes Building, I managed to disguise myself as Mr Deane, who I knew was due into Millennium radio tonight to talk about his plans for the post-Christmas slump. Mummy said I had him down to a tee (although I had to watch Emmerdale four times to get the accent right - Kim Tate was in leather trousers. Felt a bit funny again) until I realised I was late and rushed out of the house to catch the bus into town. "If you keep moving at that sort of speed, NO-ONE will believe it's him!" she shouted after me.

Eventually though I managed to make it to Millenium Radio (had to pay a FULL FARE on the bus for the first time in my life! Serves me right for wearing 6" platform shoes. Why does Mr Deane have to be so tall?) and marched through the main doors. The burly security guard said "Evening, Brian!" as I headed towards the recording studios, but seconds later I was distracted by a minor kerfuffle behind me. "Brian Deane my eye! HE's already here!" I heard a gruff voice say. "YOU'RE just an imposter coated in make-up from that little shop in the Forbes buliding!" At first I thought I had been rumbled more noisily than Mr Stamp's stomach, but imagine my surprise when I turned around to see the REAL Mr Deane being manhandled out of the building by the same burly security guard! "Eh up lad, I AM the real Brian Deane! I'll go to t'foot of our stairs!" I heard him saying, but all to no avail. I turned on my heel to head up into the studios but was shocked to hear a disturbingly familiar voice coming around the corner...

"Brian, you big Yorkshire pudding!" said Mr Robson, ominously. "I thought I'd find you here. Brownlegs has gone down with terminal enthusiasm so the show's been cancelled tonight, but I believe it's you on duty with the old ceremonial wooden claw! Now come on - Ground Force is on in half an hour and I've got a REALLY itchy lower back..."

And with that I was frogmarched back to the Riverside Stadium to scratch Mr Robson's back vigorously while we both watched Charlie Dimmock bending over her begonias. Felt even funnier than I ever have before!!! I really must go and see the club doctor sometime...

Love, Craig xxx

Be The Boss

A career in football, once the heady days of Cup Finals and winners medals all over the place are at an end, invariably leads to management.

This can be a traumatic transition, as a player crosses the line from being 'one of us' to become 'one of them.' The shin pads and tracky top are replaced by Armani suits and disgusting ties. The wild nights of birds and booze are replaced by wild nights of psychology and tactical assessment. And the flash 2 seater sports car is replaced by the flash...er...2 seater sports car.

A good manager must be skilled in all areas of man management. He has to be seen as 'the gaffer' whilst remaining 'one of the lads.' He will be his own man and at the same time be the Chairman's plaything. His CV can span many years and many clubs. Success one day can turn to failure the next. In such an instance, he must find the inner strength to accept failure, deal with the pain, negotiate a seven-figure settlement, and move on.

Managers are very complex individuals who learn to cope with tremendous pressure, and develop new skills. For instance, not only do they have to pick the team, but also type it out really neatly and stick it on the notice board.

Football has a long tradition of 'colourful' managers (i.e. useless at their job but good value for interviews). It has long been assumed that great players make great managers. Of course this is a load of rubbish. For example, in his brief tenure at Preston North End, Bobby Charlton did for football management what Salmon Rushdie later did for racial harmony.

There was a time when a manager only needed to be able to say, "Well played Nifty me old cock sparra!" once a week to get the best out of his playing staff. However, a modern day manager must now command extensive language and diplomacy skills to get his message across. Typically, in any half time pep talk, he will need to shout "You useless piece of s**t!" in around 26 languages - although many avoid this tedious phrasebook referencing by simply banging players on the head with a cup.

The manager is also the focal point for the media and their constant campaign of terror. The post-game press conference is a test for even the most seasoned press manipulator, especially after a 6-0 home pasting where 3 of his players were wrongly sent off and the ref shouted "Get in!" whenever the opposition scored. With the FA having set stringent rules on abusing officials, the manager may well wish to comment along the lines of "that referee is the spawn of Satan and should be burned at the stake," but he is left with little to offer aside from "we were a tad naïve."

In short, his position is unenviable for many reasons. Despite the perks afforded by huge salaries, spanking cars and luxurious houses, a run of poor form will lead to a feeding frenzy of media lust as they sense a sacking. Of course should his future be in any doubt, he can draw strength from his Chairman issuing him a 'vote of confidence.' Sadly, this is normally followed by the issuing of this month's 'Situations Vacant.'

Ian Nesbitt

You Are The Manager

Having overviewed the role of a football club boss, and decided what a complete doss it must be, here's a chance to assess your own leadership style and see if you'd be heading for Premiership glory or the Betty Ford Clinic. Choose carefully now...

1. Losing 2-0 at home with 15 minutes left and down to ten men. Your centre forward hasn't had a shot all day and the midfield hasn't completed a pass. Your bench includes two forwards, one of whom has been warming up for almost an hour, and a gifted midfielder who continually comes on and scores crucial goals. What do you do?
A. Nothing.
B. Change both forwards, bring on your gifted midfielder, change your 5-3-1 to 3-4-2, score twice in a minute and wrap up victory in injury time with a 20-yard volley.
C. Take the forward off and bring on an unknown continental right back - go to 6 at the back to make sure they don't get another. Pray that teams around you lose as well. Start planning a verbal assault on the ref for sending off your star man.

2. The transfer market is aglow with activity. You have £20m to spend and your side is crying out for a quality striker, pace in midfield, a wingback and a centre half. You have a squad of 40, half of whom are over 35 years old. How do you balance the books?
A. Try and tempt Platty and Hoddle out of management and get on the phone to Frank Worthington. And surely George Best has one more season in him.
B. Sell all the dead wood; bring in Batistuta, Cannavaro, Albertini and Rivaldo. Win the Premiership, FA Cup, League Cup, Super Cup and World Club Championship. And remember not to buy Chris Sutton.
C. Buy Duncan Ferguson despite him collapsing during the medical.

3. You get thumped 8-0 at home in the Cup by 3rd Division strugglers. Your team plays like a bunch of tarts and your star men are all in rehab clinics. How do you respond?
A. Do nothing. They'll come good.
B. Accept the blame for a poor performance and resolve to put things right. Spend the following week analysing weaknesses. Start working on new tactics, defensive strategy, fitness levels and dead ball situations. Concentrate on winning the league and beat Sunderland 29-0 away to clinch the title and condemn them to relegation.
C. Blame the ref. Oh, and Shearer. And Ferguson.

4. What do you take to the game?
A. Er, the team. Oh, and some sandwiches.
B. Videos of the opposition's last 10 games, opposition player by player analysis, tactics sheets, pre match motivational speech, and post game press conference notes.
C. Vast experience. And the knowledge that I'm always right.

5. Your team makes its worst start to the season for 40 years. You have assembled the worst defence in the known world and leave your star striker on the bench. Having eventually brought him on, you blame him for losing you the game. Who do you think is responsible for this state of affairs?
A. No one really. It's just one of those things.
B. You. Your team selections have proven to be misguided and there is no spirit among the players. But once you've sorted out the teething troubles, restored the pride in the players, made a couple of key signings and implemented training and tactical improvements, the team will be unbeatable.
C. Those bloody referees. How are you possibly expected to legislate for them constantly giving decisions against your team? And these star strikers - you were winning 'til they came on, with their public profiles and big salaries. It's a disgrace and who do they think they are and anyway it's your ball and you're going home.

Answers:
A. Not really got the hang of this management lark, have you? Not too strong at making decisions and not really up to speed with the demands of the modern game. Try getting a job as an ITV summariser.
B. Wow! You really have this management thing licked. You can see the failings, take responsibility for the team and will have the respect of fellow managers and fans alike. You will probably sign a lucrative new contract or go on to coach in Europe where you continue to learn before returning to England to lead the national side to World Cup glory.
C. Sorry, Ruud. Don't call us...

Ian Nesbitt

The FMTTM Millannual

players in the moon
JOHN HICKTON

John Hickton, born 24/9/44, debut 24/9/66 v Workington, last game 25/4/78 v West Ham 458/24 app. 185 goals.

WHAT DO YOU REMEMBER ABOUT YOUR FIRST GAME?

JH: It was against Workington, I was playing centre half. The forward I was marking scored 2 in the first 5 minutes. We got a penalty which I scored, and we ended up winning 3-2 This was early in the 3rd Division season, the first time Boro had been in the 3rd Division. They were near the bottom of the division when I joined, we got better as the year went on and ended up getting promoted. It was the team of John O'Rourke, David Chadwick, Gordon Jones, Eric McMordie, Dicky Rooks, Bill Gates, people like that.

WHAT'S YOUR BEST MEMORY?

JH: The Ayresome Angel days in the 3rd Division, when the support built up from virtually nothing to 40,000, on the night we clinched promotion against Oxford. As far as goals go, my favourite is one against Man Utd. I chipped it over Stepney into the far corner in a Cup game at Ayresome Park.

WHAT DO YOU REMEMBER ABOUT YOUR LAST GAME?

JH: Nothing. I can't even remember who it was against.

G-R-E-A-T BORO MOMENTS

TERRY COCHRANE

Bicycle Kick v Swansea
Jan 3rd 1981

Tricky winger Terry Cochrane was a real crowd pleaser in the great Boro team of John Neal. A club record buy for £238, 000, TC went on to win 19 of his 26 Northern Ireland caps while with the Boro.

He tortured many a First Division opponent down the right flank as he headed towards the by-line providing deadly service for prolific strikers Micky Burns and then Bosco Jankovic.

Here we see Terry recreating his crowning moment. It's the famous bicycle kick captured by Match of the Day cameras in the 5-0 demolition of Swansea at the Vetch Field on a cold January day in 1981. In the words of MoTD commentator David Coleman "Oh I say.... what a goal, what a GOAL!!"

The Day I Met......

You worship them on the pitch, you may have even set up a shrine to them on the bedroom/living room wall. They're stars and they are not mortal like you or I. I'm talking about Boro footballers past and present. But what happens when you chance upon one of our Boro heroes in a real life situation?
Chris Bartley and **Bob Fischer** get all nostalgic and recall that starstruck first encounter of the Boro kind.

> THE CAST: CRAIG JOHNSTON AND TONY McANDREW.
> THE SCENE: SOUTH PARK SIXTH FORM COLLEGE DO AT THE MADHOUSE NIGHTCLUB DECEMBER 1980

There has been a lot of drivel written about rites of passage and that troubled journey from boy to man. In Hollywood, it's all that nonsense about watching your best friend die as he drives a car off a cliff. Another scenario is having an affair with your best friend's mother. But as that learned Mancunian Morrissey once said, "this says nothing to me about my life". No, forget that, and all talk about crafty fags and adolescent fumblings behind the bike shed, in my day in Middlesbrough a boy becomes a man when he gets into the Madison for the first time and chats to a Boro player like he is his best mate. In my life, this unique event happened in December 1980.

I can remember the build up as though it was yesterday. The endless wait on the Madhouse stairs. The first glance of the neanderthal bouncer who will decide your fate. I can remember the feeling of exultation as I was allowed in to progress to the next stage and the ritual of handing in your coat to the cloakroom girl. Once again it is a ritual you must observe - whether you want to hand in your coat or not. You hand in your coat, get your raffle ticket and guard that ticket as if it was your winning lottery ticket. This is essential, because all men know it is impossible to describe your jacket at the best of times, never mind after a couple of pints. Being afflicted with colour blindness, I can't even remember the colour half the time.

After getting into the Madhouse, everything goes rapidly downhill. You realise you only have enough money for one watered down pint, the music is execrable and the DJ is the type of bloke who thinks Dave Lee Travis is genuinely funny. It's 10.30 and you have to stay there until 2 o'clock because you're sharing a taxi with two lads from Normanby. Yes, everything you wished and hoped for turns out to be totally crap, and you've blown a month's worth of pocket money. You don't even get the chance to snog anyone because you look so ridiculously young.

But on that December night, redemption came in the unlikely guise of Tony McAndrew, the erstwhile captain of the Boro team, and Craig Johnston. I don't know what prompted me to do it, but buoyed up by the type of confidence that only alcohol can provide, I summoned up the courage to have what is commonly known as footy banter. My first target Tony Mc was obviously bored and he made his apologies and headed for the dance floor, to dance with one of the lasses from our sixth form. But Craig Johnston seemed a much nicer person. He stood talking to me for ages and he fielded all my numerous questions about our chances in the league, FA Cup etc, seemed to think Tony Mc was a bit of a git and he seemed as isolated as me in some ways. He wasn't drinking and in the light of some of the comments he made in his autobiography a few years back, the Boro first team made him feel like a total outsider, the stupid surf dude from Australia. So we spoke for a good hour or so and then he left and for a brief moment I felt that I'd spoken to him not as a fawning boy but an equal, as a young man. Yes, I'd made a big leap into manhood and it felt cool. Of course, it would have been much better if, the moment he left the

Madhouse, I'd got fixed up with some girl from college, but you can't win them all. As I stood in the legendary cloakroom queue listening to Herb Alpert's easy listening Bacharach-scribed classic "This Guy's in Love with You", I knew one day my time would come. My snog would come later but at least that night, Matthew, I had stars in my eyes.

Chris Bartley

> THE CAST: JON GITTENS, BERNIE SLAVEN AND IN FACT THE ENTIRE BORO FIRST-TEAM SQUAD. THE SCENE: THE MALL NIGHTCLUB, STOCKTON, 1992

A matter of days before Christmas 1992, at the end of a riotous bar crawl around Stockton High Street, my friends and I ended up in the giddy auspices of The Mall for a gig by 80s cabaret ska-fiends Bad Manners. Just before the band went on stage, and strongly under the influence of bad lager and festive spirit, I was shocked to find myself suddenly trapped in the middle of a large crowd of fancy-dressed revellers, all sporting wide-lapelled shirts, flares and platform shoes. I was even more shocked to realise, seconds later, that every last damn one of them was a Boro first-team squad member - even the half-naked bloke in the ludicrous chest wig was none other than our own Living Leg End Bernie Slaven and on closer inspection it, ulp, wasn't a chest wig after all! Anyroadup the band appeared and much nutty-dancing ensued but the highspot of the evening was undoubtedly when, during a break in the set, a huge jive-walking Superfly strutted over in my direction, looked me quizzically in the eyes then reached out and tugged hard on my (admittedly substantial) ginger sideboards. "Ow!" I shouted back with shock and surprise. "What the bloody hell was that for?" "Sorry mate," replied Jon Gittens - for it was he - "I thought they were stick-on ones, just like mine" and with that he staggered away and got off with some girl on the dance floor, and I finished off the night bouncing around to "Lip Up Fatty" with Tommy Wright and Alan Kernaghan. Happy days.

Those very sideboards, that very night, December 1992

Bob Fischer

And there's more...

I once saw Lennie Lawrence in Yarm with a puzzled look upon his face. Jokingly I said "Hiya Lennie - what's up, lost yer car? Hee hee." To which he replied "Yes - I think it might be up there somewhere, splutter, cough, cough!" He left shortly afterwards.

Mike McBride

I remember when I was about fourteen playing tennis in Ropner Park with my mate, and Willie Maddren and George Smith were playing on the next court (could you imagine present day players playing in a public park?). We only had one crappy bald tennis ball between us and Willie came over and gave us a couple of his pristine Slazengers. I was a devoted fan from that moment on. A really nice guy. Why did it have to happen to him?

Andy, Stockton

Gary Pallister used to call for my younger brother when they were at Blakeston School together, I used to open the door, call him a lanky B**tard and hit him cos he had an annoying way of knocking, he used to flinch every time I saw him. At an away game a few years later I remember him coming near to the Boro fans in the warm up to retrieve a ball, I shouted to him that he was a lanky b**tard.....For one moment I swear he flinched.

Colin

The Way They Were

Clean-shaven and crop-haired may be Robbo's current style, but back in '81 at WBA he was without a doubt that rare and special thing... a Terry McDermott wannabee! Ladies and gentlemen...

Bryan "Robbo" Robson
Nice hair, sir!

My claim to fame is sneaking Higgy in through the back doors of the Manchester hotel where I worked at 2am, the night before we played Man City. Had to get him through the back door as Pickering and McQueen were still propping up the hotel bar near the front door. Nice bloke mind, and he signed my shirt, shame he had a stinker the next day! Good luck Higgy!

Doug

Don't know whether this tops it or not, but as a 13 or 14 year old or so, along with a mate (Stephen McAndrew) I interviewed John Hickton in his home in Nunthorpe for our school (Frederick Nattrass Secondary Modern) magazine. Wish I had kept a copy!

Pete

And now for the Gazza section...

Just before last Christmas, who was on the train going back to London with MSSers from the West Ham game? Paul Gascoigne. He looked fit and healthy, had a great time, signing hundreds of autographs for West Ham fans and chatted for ages with anyone who wanted to talk to him. You won't read this in the tabloids but everyone who met him was bowled over by the bloke. Pass the word on.

Geoff

I was in Vilamoura in Spain during the summer and saw Gazza several times around the place. As the story is now out I would like to say my impression was that the guy was just on holiday with a few mates having a good time. Okay he was having a drink but so was everyone else, in the same way most of us do on holiday. I must have been in the bar when some of the pictures in the Sun were taken as I recognise them, I had my picture taken with Gazza later that evening and he certainly was not p*ssed! In Gazza's defence I thought he was a great ambassador for football, he was always being stopped by people for a handshake or autograph or picture and every time he obliged happily. Also I spoke to a few of his mates and they are just regular blokes who happen to have a very famous friend, they are certainly not a bunch of sycophants who hang on his every word.

Brian

Thanks to Phil Davies for trawling his internet archives to put this together from the Boro (internet) maliing list.

My mam met Gazza. He was at someone's house in the road, and the neighbours all turned out to see him, apparently it ended up as a street party with Gazza driving up and down the cul-de sac waving to the cheering crowds!

Neville

I would like to reply to the newspaper report (September, 1999). In the report it stated that Paul Gascoigne was drunk and had to be helped out of Ryhope Workmen's club. As I was the club doorman on that night, I would like to give my account of what happened. Paul Gascoigne came into the club with a few family and friends, but not with Jimmy "Five Bellies", as was reported, and from the moment he came in people were coming up to him to ask for autographs.
The same happened when he got to the concert room, but he signed everybody's without complaining, he later went on to have a great night with family and friends, he had a few drinks and danced until he had to go home. He even turned round to everybody and thanked them for a great night, his father then went outside to make sure his taxi had arrived and at no time did he need any help to leave the club or get into his taxi.

S. H., Ryhope

Hey Chrissy Man, Here's your Mullet juice

Gazza on Hair Care

Our Willie...

Some five and a half years ago I received a message from my trusty Citroen that the suspension hydraulics were on the point of collapse. I was told many years ago that the best way of getting shot of a swarm of midgies was to leave them with someone else, and so with this as my moral guide I headed off to my local Toyota dealer.
Strolling nonchalantly around the forecourt trying not to let my desperation show, I was spotted. The salesman was heading purposefully towards me with something of a swagger. "Hang on a minute," I thought as he got closer, "I know you". And sure enough, it was Willie Maddren.
After the usual hoohaa associated with the buying of a motor, I finally left the garage several meetings later with my shiny new car. We'd had a few good chats with Willie during the process, about the Jack Charlton era, about Jack's reluctance to buy a good striker, about Phil Boersma's sending off on his debut against Bury in the Cup, about the new foreigner at the Boro (we'd just signed Jaime Moreno) and about Willie's time as manager, his sports shop venture and his transition into car salesman.
One thing that struck me at the time was that, as Willie hadn't taken delivery of his business cards, he handed me a blank one on which he'd written his name. I thought it strange because his handwriting was shaky, rather like the signature of an old man.... About eight months later Willie announced to the world that he was suffering from Motor Neurone disease.
Fast forward to January, 1998, and I was working for Hillprint, the designers and printers of the Boro programme and the Willie Maddren autobiography. I was asked to go to a meeting at Willie's house with a Hillprint director. I went in to meet Willie, who by this time was in a wheel chair, unable to raise his hands and only able to talk with a great deal of difficulty.
"Ah, Hello Mr Wilson," he said, "How's your car". I was not a little taken aback by this as it had been nearly four years since I'd had any contact with him. "Fine," I said. "A red Carina, wasn't it?"
After the business of the meeting I asked Willie how he'd remembered me. He said "I remember your wife, too. Jan. And your kids. She was expecting wasn't she?" Wilson counts backwards on his fingers. "Yes, she was. How can you remember all this?" "I was trying to sell you a bigger car."

Alex Wilson

Marooned on Moon Island

PAUL ARMSTRONG (MotD)

FIVE MATCH VIDEOS

Two videos that exist; 101 Great Boro Goals and The Bernie Slaven Story.
And three that don't; 1973/74 season's highlights, The 1996/7 Coca Cola Cup run (video ends after 117 minutes at Wembley), The 1996/7 FA Cup run (video ends after 41 seconds at Wembley).

MEMORABILIA

I've got a signed photo of Juninho celebrating his diving header against Chelsea on my office wall. It's a fantastic picture of a great moment and I got him to sign it when I went to the team hotel in FA Cup Final week. It's the only time I've been unprofessional enough to ask for an autograph while I've worked here, but I'm glad I did.

I'm also quite attached to my replica 73/74 home and away shirts - I think we should always have a white hoop on the red shirt, and I always loved that Inter Milan away kit. It's probably just a sad sign of my age.

BORO PERSON

I'd like to talk to whoever scores our first winning goal at Wembley. I think it's too late for it to be me now, though I'm quite fond of talking to myself about Boro and probably would do for hours on end on a desert island.

FIRST MATCH

A. Boro 5 Norwich 0 (Downing, Hickton(2), McIlmoyle, Laidlaw) Feb 6th 1971. A glorious introduction to Ayresome Park. I particularly remember Norwich's helpless keeper Kevin Keelan who looked like the bloke from the Milk Tray advert. My next game was a 4-0 win over Swindon, leading me to believe that we always thrashed the opposition... Ah, the innocence of youth...

BEST MEMORY

The promotions, particularly at Stamford Bridge in 1988. To bounce back from bankruptcy and the 3rd division in two seasons was incredible. Being Boro we couldn't go up the easy way; we'd messed up automatic promotion at home to Leicester and ended up in the play-offs. The away end at Chelsea was miles from the pitch, and the second half when we were under siege at the far end was almost unwatchable; every corner looked like a certain goal.
Mowbray and Pallister and co. held on and I embarrassed myself by getting emotional at the final whistle, more from relief than anything else. It was even worth being showered with lumps of concrete and kept in for over an hour afterwards.
Shame we went straight back down again, and that Chelsea came back to haunt us (repeatedly)

WORST MEMORY

Without question Heskey's equaliser at Wembley - I still feel ill just thinking about it. I suppose not knowing if we still had a club or not in 1986 wasn't much fun, either. Oh, and watching us concede a penalty and lose 1-0 to nine men at Crystal Palace in 1984 was pretty lousy, too. Then there was Officer Dibble's cartoon keeping at QPR last year... But it still has to be that horrible, undeserved, slow motion trickle over the line that deprived us of a first-ever trophy and sent a potentially glorious season spinning off down the pan. Thanks a lot, Emile.

MOONSTRUCK

Katie Medd (Meddical)

MY FIRST EVER BORO MATCH was in the 1995/96 season (the first season at the Riverside Stadium) against QPR. My season ticket hadn't come yet so I had to sit in the West Stand Upper. Normally, when people go to their first Boro match they end up getting thrashed, but, oh no, not when I went. It was a very memorable match and I don't think I will ever forget it. In the first half we got a penalty when Barmby was brought down in the area. Craig Hignett, of course, converted it. In the second half, Barmby was brought down again and penalty awarded, but this time Jan Fjortoft decided that he wanted to have a go. Foolishly Craig Hignett let him........he missed. He hit the cross bar and couldn't get near it to try and convert it a second time as it fell straight into the keepers arms. We won 1-0 and that was it, I was hooked.
I know four years isn't very long to have been supporting Boro (compared to some people) but in the those four years so much has happened.

BY FAR THE BEST MOMENT AS A BORO FAN was when we got promoted after beating Oxford 4-1. My all-time favourite player Craig Hignett scored twice and we beat Sunderland by 1 point. There was a massive party going on in Middlesbrough. In one pub Peter Reid was on a big screen talking to Sky after finding out that they hadn't been promoted because we had won. As he spoke we sang to the screen, "Peter Reid's got a tellytubbie's head." Along with a few other versions, yes, I'm sure you know which ones I am talking about! I also thoroughly enjoyed watching the Sunderland fans cry when they found out. It was a brilliant day.

THE WORST TIME being a Boro fan was the week when we were relegated at Elland Road against Leeds and then beaten 2-0 in the F.A Cup Final against Chelsea. A 1-1 draw against Leeds just wasn't good enough and we were relegated along with Sunderland and Notts Forest. In the cup final Festa had had a perfectly fine goal ruled out for offside which could possibly have changed the match. Even if it hadn't, at least it would've given us something to cheer about. I left as soon as the final whistle was blown, I was off, I just couldn't bear to watch them lift the cup. It was a long trip back to Middlesbrough. I was inconsolable.
Four years is just the beginning of a long time supporting the finest team in the world and although they put us through every emotion known to man, Boro are my team and I am prepared to stand by them through thick and thin for life.

C'MON BORO!!!!!!

The FMTTM Millannual

RONNIE DICKS (1950s)
Ronnie played all over the park,
In 350 Boro appearances,
Centre forward, inside left,
And a few goal line clearances.

The FMTTM Millannual

Get Your Shirts On for the ....

Clothes maketh the man – and why should the Boro be any different? Now that we we've got a white and purple away kit (Silk Cut, anyone?) inflicted on us, it seemed a good time to examine the great kits the Boro have worn in the last twenty years, and also nominate the very worst kit we ever wore. Here we go, starting in the distant depths of the past when Jack Charlton chose the team for tonnage rather than skill:

1973-74 – Charlton Classic
Manufacturer – Bukta (although you can get repros from Screeching Parrot and Toffs)
What did it look like? – Smart. After years of plain anonymous red, we got this glorious piece of the shirt maker's art. Bright red with the famous white band at chest height, red shorts with the number on, red socks. For the first time since the 1930's, Boro had a shirt that was distinct from any other teams'.
Was it lucky? – God yes. This shirt got us promoted by a record margin, and saw us stay in the top flight for the longest period in modern times. To many people, this was the classic Boro shirt.
What was the away shirt like? – Another classic, the famous blue and black stripes, modelled on the Inter Milan shirt reputedly because Stan Anderson was an admirer, much as Don Revie changed the Leeds kit to all-white in the 1950's because of his love of Real Madrid.
Marks out of 10 - 10

1978 - Adidas chest band
Manufacturer – Adidas
What did it look like? – Like a red Adidas shirt with long sleeves and the famous white band. Even Billy Ashcroft could look good in this number, one of the few Boro shirts that could be called sexy (except when Alan Ramage was wearing it).
Was it lucky? – It was OK. We normally managed mid-table mediocrity in this one, and never dipped out of the top flight.
What was the away shirt like? – All blue. No band, no nothing. We looked like Ipswich. And it had a horrible broad white hang-glider collar on it. Boring, boring Boro.
Marks out of 10 - 9

1988 - Bib front
Manufacturer – Skill
What did it look like? – Bright red polyester and tight, like, really TIGHT, with a strange white bib-like patch on the chest. The first Boro shirt made in-house, by little-known North Ormesby sweatshop merchants Skill Leisure. Worn with distinction by Pally, Coops, Mogga, Slav and a legion of adult Boro fans, wearing repro shirts in large numbers for the first time. Sponsored for a nominal sum by Heritage Hampers (the deal was rumoured to be a Christmas hamper for each team member, and two for Gary Hamilton)
Was it lucky? – Lucky like a yo-yo. Got us into the first division, then out again, then to Wembley, where Chelsea beat us. A perfect shirt for Boro's fortunes in the later 80's.
What was the away shirt like? – As above, but the white bits were red and vice-versa. OK if you liked that sort of thing (and, once again, *incredibly* tight).
Marks out of 10 – 6

1994 - first Errea
Manufacturer – Errea
What did it look like? – After a horrible effort by Admiral the year before, Italian shirtmeisters Errea took over the repro kit contract, and brought out this classic little number. Still seen in fairly significant numbers at the Riverside. Red with a dark blue collar and cuffs, simple and stylish. Only let down by the shirt sponsor, Dickens. However, we only got a dicking off Luton while we wore them, so there.
Was it lucky? – We won the First Division Championship after a very dodgy period after Christmas in it, so I suppose that yes, it must have been. The last shirt ever worn at Ayresome Park.

What was the away shirt like? – Bloody horrible. Two shades of green with a thin yellow stripe – we looked like marrows. Especially Jamie Pollock, who played like a marrow as well.

Marks out of 10 – 5 (10 for the home, 1 for the away)

1997 Wembley
Manufacturer – Errea
What did it look like – A bit like the 1994 shirt with a bit more white in it
Was it lucky? – well, we got to Wembley while we were wearing it, so it's got to be sort of lucky. On the other hand, we lost all three cups that year (League, FA and Staying Up) so in another way, it wasn't. Simple, classy and durable (you still see thousands every Saturday) Also brought out in a special Coca-Cola Finalists rip off issue (same shirt, different badge)
What was the away shirt like – A classic. White with a blue cross and the sacred letters BORO down one of the arms. Probably the best away top to come out since the 'Inter Milan' look of the early 70's. Just right for Juninho to net Boro's greatest goal against the Mancs in, one horrible bank holiday Monday a few years ago.

Marks out of 10 - 7

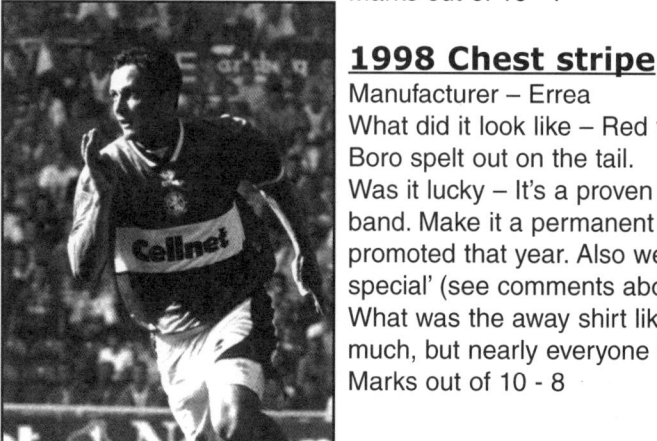

1998 Chest stripe
Manufacturer – Errea
What did it look like – Red with the classic Boro white chestband, a neat collar and Boro spelt out on the tail.
Was it lucky – It's a proven fact – we always get promoted when we wear the white band. Make it a permanent feature, Mr Gibson. It was bloody lucky, as we were to get promoted that year. Also went to Wembley with us in a money-spinning 'cup final special' (see comments above).
What was the away shirt like – Sort of blue with a big white vertical stripe. I didn't like it much, but nearly everyone else did, so what do I know.
Marks out of 10 - 8

AND NOW THE WORST...........
There have been some contenders for this category – the Admiral shirt we wore in the first year of the premiership, all the plain red efforts of the 1960's that made us look exactly like Liverpool or Man U (but not play like them, unfortunately). However, for my money the worst has to be:

The 1984 'Arsenal lookalike kit
Manufacturer – Bodgit and Scarper, Market Traders, North Ormesby
What did it look like – Like an Arsenal shirt if Arsenal had been forced to buy their kit off doggy market. See the picture in 'Boro's Best' on the Heine Otto page.
Was it lucky – Malcolm Allison. David Currie. Double Demotion. This shirt. You get the message?
What was the away shirt like – I honestly have no idea, and as any examples have fallen apart long since, I'm sure no one else has either.
Marks out of ten – Nothing, and a very low nothing too.

Rob Hymer

The FMTTM Millannual

ATTENTION ALL YOU BORO NUTS OUT THERE!!!

MUSH-TACHIO PISTACHIO

WIN £250 SEE BELOW

Look here, put down those Christmas nuts granddaddy, it's a filthy habit and you really ought to know better at your age. Cast a Pat Butchers over this ugly lot, corr blimey! It's a simple party game for all the family. All you need to do is take an eyeball at this parade of stately and not so seemly upper lip warmers and work out which Boro stars past and present were thus adorned. In other words whose is the mush in the mush-tache mamma.

Just to give you some incentive the good people from Juniper Publishing are making you an incredible offer. There is a marvellous prize of £250 for whoever can identify Boro's Hair Bear Bunch. There will be a draw live on air on Red Balls on Fire (Radio Cleveland 95FM) on Friday 28th January - so tune in and prepare to get some spending money. All entrants must submit the official coupon below, no photocopies will be accepted.

All entries to: **FLY ME TO THE MOON, Unit 7, Brentnall Centre, Brentnall Street, Middlesbrough TS1 5AP.**
Closing date (to be received) Thursday 27th January (2000)

Name _____

Address _____

_____

_____

1. _____ 6. _____
2. _____ 7. _____
3. _____ 8. _____
4. _____ 9. _____
5. _____ 10. _____

51

The FMTTM Millannual

Battle of the Boro

	Emerson	v	**Alan Foggon**
Appearances:	70 – sick Aunts Permitting		141
Style:	'Soul Glo' South American bodyguard		Workhorse
Physique:	Thighs like trees		Girth. And lots of it.
Goals:	11		50
Training:	Now and then		Rubber suit a speciality
Injuries:	Impressively few for a combative midfielder Thankfully never fell on anyone.		Cuts, bruises, broken legs he caused them to everybody.
Hobbies:	Fags. And travel.		Socialising. But only after, before and during, a match.

G-R-E-A-T BORO MOMENTS

Hickton getting closer, closer, closer....

FMTTM competition coupon

52

Players in the Moon — JOHN CRAGGS

Fly: What can you remember about your first game for Middlesbrough?

JC: My first game I believe was against Sheffield Wednesday. It was a night match we won 2-1, which was pretty good. It was always nice to play in the evenings because there was always a bit more atmosphere with the lights and everything. Stan Anderson brought me for £60 000.

Fly: That was a lot in those days, wasn't it?

JC: It was the club record buy at the time. I wasn't a regular in the first team at Newcastle but Stan came in and I jumped at the chance to get first team football, David Craig an Irish international was the regular full back and I got a chance when he was injured. I did well in the team, but when he was fit again he was put straight back in, which you can understand because he was a good player.

Fly: It was maybe unusual to break the transfer record for a defender.

JC: I suppose so but in those days there wasn't a lot of money flying about and apparently they had to sell Hughie McIlmoyle for about £50,000 to fund buying me. So he left the club and then they brought me in.

Fly: Do you remember your final game for Middlesbrough?

JC: Bobby Murdoch was the manager. I honestly can't remember the game to tell the truth.

Fly: Perhaps that sums up that period.

JC: Yes, they got relegated that season. My last game was the next season when I'd joined Newcastle and I brought a Newcastle team down for my testimonial. I went back to Newcastle for a season. Apparently when I went to Newcastle they bought John Brownlie down from Newcastle. To cut a long story short, they offered me less money on my contract, and I said no so I was entitled to a free transfer and I went to Newcastle and Boro spent £30 000 on John Brownlie and he left after 12 months. So they blew £30 000, a lot less than they would have been paying me in wages. Money was pretty tight so I don't know what their thinking was.

---

and in a packed programme tonight...

Bob Fischer cuts snippets of genius from the Boro's match programmes of yesteryear

1974: MR BYCRAFT CALVERT AND MR HILL

Before! After! Before! After! Visitors to Eatons, "Teesside's Oldest Established Furnishers and Piano Dealers" must have been peturbed on or around the 24th September 1974 to be greeted by Mr Thomas Bycraft Calvert. "A new piano, sir? Certainly! I'll just fetch our sales director Mr Hill..." (vanishes out the back for thirty seconds to re-emerge sporting a badly-fitted wig but still, blatantly, the same bloke). "Ah good day, sir, allow me to introduce myself. I'm Jack Hill, sales director here at Eatons of Parliament Road. What's that? You want to speak to Mr Calvert again? Oh bollocks, hang on then..."

The FMTTM Millannual

STRICTLY BALLROOM

During the late 1920s Herbert Chapman was the tactical mastermind behind Huddersfield Town's challenge for both the League Championship and FA Cup. He moved down to the smoke to repeat and even better his successes at Arsenal where he founded the start of a dynasty that has stretched until today, with the Highbury club still sitting pretty at the top of the domestic football tree. It was during this time that Chapman became famous for re-writing the book of football tactics, reinventing the role of centre half. He justly earned himself the epitaph of the first GREAT football manager.

Not as well known however is the story of how the great man sought to bring poetry to the beautiful game. Renowned for his forward thinking and innovations Chapman left no stone unturned in his quest for footballing perfection. In the age of pudding bowl pitches, leaden caseys and concrete shin pads Herbert was the first to go in search of a spiritual side to the sport. Initially he dabbled with religion sending forth captain Eddie Hapgood on a pilgrimage to the great northern shrines of St Mirren and St Johnstone. It was at St Mirren that Hapgood jeopardised his captaincy by dropping out of pre-season training to hang out with the beatniks of Love Street. Chapman intervened in the nick of time, spiriting Hapgood away from the sect, and forcing him to swap back his Gunners top for a Paisley shirt.

Instead of religion Herbert Chapman found solace in the art of movement and grace. As these pictures clearly show Chapman trained his troops to master the weapons of the ballroom dancefloor to bolster his Arsenal armoury. Indeed it was an instant success as the Arsenal strikeforce often mesmerised opponents with their lightning fandango. The crowds flocked to see speedy winger Ralph Birkett pasa doble before the North Bank. Our first photo shows striker Alex James leading Sunderland's Robert Thomson a merry dance, a touch of the Gay Gordons if I'm not mistaken.

The second photograph records Chapman's revolutionary "W" forward formation of Bastin, Jack and James carrying out one of their most celebrated dance manoeuvres, a quick fox-trot into a full tango. Note the complete synchronisation of movement.

Sadly the dance experiment was put to bed with the untimely death of Chapman in 1934 and thus another bold, imaginative, pioneering idea was lost to the game forever.

BRIAN CLOUGH (1960s)
Cloughie scored a goal a game,
You know that can't be bad,
A centre forward with no equal,
And a local Grove Hill lad.

THEY PLAYED FOR MIDDLESBROUGH

James Dean

James Dean will always be remembered as the star whose career was ended by a fatal high-speed crash when he was only 17. Dean played for Middlesbrough in the late 1950s, making his name as a cult winger in the same forward line as Brian Clough. He made his debut as a 16-year-old playing on the opposite wing to the tragic genius Eddie "Billie" Holliday. Although he was adored by the crowd Dean had more than his share of disputes with manager Bob Dennison and became known as the "Rebel without a clause (in his contract)."

He was a fleet footed ball player whose laid back style of play was once described by reporter Rob Rayerson as having "a quality of tragic innocence." It was this sense of innocence that led to him being dubbed the "First Teenager" by his skipper Bill Harris.

Dean was a giant to the Boro fans, many of whom copied his "classic" Boro look of the open neck shirt, rolled down socks and of course trademark "501" shorts. £5.0.1d being the price of the shorts from Jack Hatfield's.

His fame soon spread and he was chosen to represent England "B" on their tour of East Eden when he was only 17. Whilst on tour young James Dean once more courted controversy, the national press exposing his affair with England masseur Ricky Hudson. This only served to increase Dean's mystique.

Tragically though, midway through the following season, Dean's life ended during a FA Cup-tie with Burton Swifts. Racing down the wing at an incredible speed he put in a centre but was unable to stop and he continued his run through the Bob End and into the catering stall at the back, where he was eventually halted. Unfortunately the impact caused a pork pie to fall from the top shelf and strike him on the head, killing him instantly. Fittingly Dean had lived and died by his motto, "run fast cross early" and supporters can only imagine what heights the young man might have reached if it had not been for that unusually crusty pie.

Postcript: One of the most heart-warming moments of last season was Bryan Robson's signing of James Dean's love-child Brian. It's very comforting to know that the Middlesbrough team will be carrying a spark of that rebellious genius into the next millennium.

Miniature G

---

marooned on moon island
IAN PAYNE TYNE TEES

FIVE VIDEOS FOR MOON ISLAND

1. a) Boro v Luton 30/4/95 2-1 Hendrie 2

Farewell to Ayresome Park. One of those "I was there" occasions. Hell of a day - we were on-air live all through the afternoon. A great programme to work on.

b) Tranmere v Boro 7/5/95 1-1 Fjortoft

Into the Premiership at Prenton Park. Up as Champions - the lap of honour - soaked in champagne in the dressing room post-match - a brilliant afternoon.

c) Juninho's arrival 3/11/95

I know it's not a match - but the video of the day Juninho arrived makes excellent viewing. Front page and back page news at the Riverside. The atmosphere was tremendous - schoolkids and fans of all ages gave the Brazilian an unbelievable welcome. I got a real buzz out of covering the event for Tyne Tees news.

d) Boro v Leicester Coca Cola Cup Final Wembley 1997 1-1 Ravanelli.

The sun shone, Wembley Way was filled with red and white - only the result spoiled the day. But a Cup Final is always a magic occasion.

e) Boro v Ipswich 2/5/81 2-0 Jankovic 2

My masochistic tendencies made me pick this one. It's a Boro game which will haunt me forever. You see, my team is Ipswich Town - and, with just two matches to go, we were so close to winning the title. We finished second to Aston Villa. Thanks Bosco.

MEMORABILIA

I have a 'Player of the Year Awards invitation' signed by Juninho on the night that he picked up the award. Who knows - perhaps I'll get another one in May.

BORO PERSON

John Hendrie - a good laugh, and a top bloke.

Deep in the legend of Middlesbrough Football Club lie great players, great goals and great performances. Deeper still lie some absolutely monumental cock-ups. On a club level the greatest mistake of all time must have been the failure to turn up at Blackburn in December 1996 which cost us 3 points and our place in the Premiership. On an individual level, though, what could be more disastrous and humiliating than the ultimate howler - signing for Sunderland? Well, perhaps putting the ball into your own net ranks just about as low as that and at the Boro we've had some classics that will live in the memory no matter how much Boro TV might ignore them. So - in the parlance of SkyTV and numerous cheaply made videos widely available in the shops and presented by a variety of second rate football bandwagon jumping daytime television so-called celebrities - we present the fmttm guide to Boro's best boobs, bloopers, cock-ups, fowl-ups, gaffes and glookers (OK, I made the last one up).

GARY PALLISTER v Newcastle

Let's start with a big name, not to mention a big fella. After nigh on 10 years of winning enough trophies at Manchester United to justify opening his own silver polish factory, Gary Pallister returned to the Boro at the same time as we returned to the top flight. As a mere slip of a lad, however, with only a couple of England caps to his name, Pally was guilty of a most horrendous blunder at St James's Park. With our youthful bunch of local lads, Boro climbed from Division 3 back into Division 1 and started the season well. In November came the much anticipated clash with the Geordies, renewing old rivalries and Boro fully expected to win. What followed was a complete nightmare courtesy of the Brazilian layabout Mirandinha, but it was big Gary Pallister who set United on their way to a 3-0 win by soaring like an eagle to plant a perfect header past Stephen Pears from 12 yards out which gave the keeper no chance. Less than 12 months later we sold him for a then British record fee, surely a shrewd piece of work by Sir Brucie Rioch.

TONY MOWBRAY v Everton

As Boro clambered from the abyss of liquidation we took on Everton in a thrilling series of cup ties in the days before penalty shoot outs, when a goalden goal was simply a kind of football lottery ticket or an overused Evening Gazette pun. Anyway, Boro managed a 1-1 draw at Everton, that brought the league champions back to Ayresome for a heart-stopping 2-2 thriller. Back at Goodison for the second replay we fought like tigers once more and at one goal apiece the tie looked set for extra time once more. But no, for up stepped skipper Tony Mowbray, "a colossus" in the words of Rioch, to settle the match once and for all. An Everton break down the right saw an innocuous cross into the box head for Mogga. With nimble footwork he adjusted his position and side footed the ball past that man Pears before collapsing in a heap like a hedgehog caught in headlights - a classic moment featured on the back pages of most newspapers the following day.

NICKY MOHAN v Swindon

Although this game wasn't as high profile as the previous two it was no less comical and completes a triumvirate of centre halves own goals from the late 1980s a decade which brought us Duran Duran, Howard Jones and Steve

57

Spriggs. Pallister had recently been sold and Boro were struggling in the 2nd Division, not least to find a reasonable replacement. Young Nicky Mohan was given a try and responded in style with Boro 1-0 down to Swindon at Ayresome Park and struggling to put 2 passes together. Late on Ronnie Glavin went down the left wing and attempted to cross to an unmarked Duncan Shearer. The pass was nowhere near Shearer but it mattered little as Mohan stretched to slide the ball expertly past the static Kevin Poole (Pears was out injured due to a mysterious illness linked to the abnormal number of own goals he was conceding).

Mohan stretched to slide the ball expertly past the static kevin poole

PAUL WILKINSON v Luton

The new era of Bryan Robson had dawned - and if anything this match showed that it wasn't likely to be any better than the others. Boro crashed to a 5-1 defeat at Kenilworth Road thanks to a Wilko brace. Always a handful in the air, Wilkinson's team-mates could only watch as the lanky striker first leapt to power a downward header Pallister-like into the bottom corner. Later in the half he neatly deflected a weak volley to totally wrong foot poor Stephen Pears. This turned out to be Pears' final game for Boro and he was eventually forced into retirement suffering from the little known 'own goal syndrome'. After years of hard labour under Lennie Lawrence, Wilko's powers were on the wane at this stage of his career, so much so that several weeks after the Luton game the entire crowd audibly groaned as he stepped up to take a match-winning penalty against Swindon (he still scored).

CHRIS MORRIS v Sheff Wed

Morris's spell on Teesside was prone to the odd mishap, but this ranks as one of the most explosive own goals of the lot. Relegation-bound Boro were 3 goals up at Hillsborough, before Wednesday pulled one back through Chris Bart-Williams. Not long after that a low cross into the box was intercepted by stand-in central defender Morris who laced it into the roof of the net, past rookie keeper Andy Collett. Fortunately, Boro held out for the remainder of the game but found themselves dumped out of the top flight courtesy of Sheffield United.

GARY PARKINSON v Leeds

Now this was a complete nightmare. Having come back from a goal down on a warm night at Elland Road it looked as though Boro might finally have won a hard earned point against Leeds, big spenders of the old 2nd division. A characteristically aimless pass was played by future film star Vinnie Jones and everybody breathed a sigh of relief as Gary Parkinson intercepted and knocked it gently back to Kevin Poole in the Boro goal, who simply had to gather the ball and kick it upfield for the referee to blow the final whistle. Sadly it didn't quite go to plan as Parkinson's back-pass looped towards Poole, reared viciously off the turf and bobbled crazily over his shoulder into the net. Boro players collapsed to the floor, Leeds fans invaded the pitch with delight and Kevin Poole's former confidence never did reappear. FIFA later banned back-passes to the goalie in order to make the game more exciting; clearly a tape of this game didn't reach their offices.

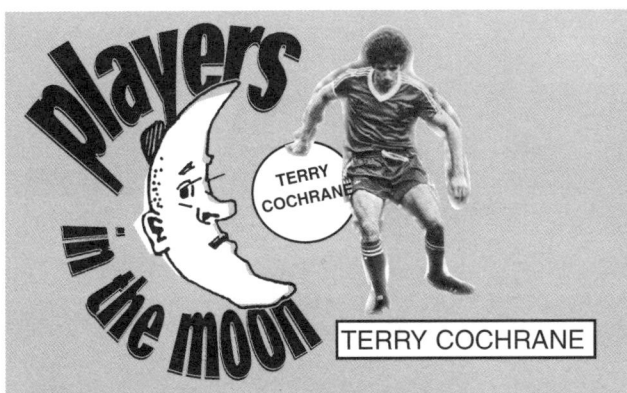

Players in the Moon

TERRY COCHRANE

DO YOU REMEMBER YOUR FIRST GAME AT BORO?
TC: I think it was against Wolves.

I THINK IT WAS NORWICH ACTUALLY ACCORDING TO THE RECORD BOOKS, WE THOUGHT IT WAS WOLVES AS WELL BEFORE WE CHECKED.
TC: (laughs) I think my brain's going at the moment. No, it was very exciting for me coming into the First Division, which was like the Premiership then. I wanted to make a good impression, and I think I did. I played the way people wanted me to at the time and it was good to play on the wing, which I was an out and out winger. You see things nowadays where they are taking away wingers for systems. Fair enough you've got to sometimes but I'm a big believer in wide play.

DO YOU REMEMBER YOUR LAST GAME?
TC: Oh no.

IT WAS WHEN MALCOLM ALLISON CAME IN, AND YOU WEREN'T PART OF HIS PLANS WERE YOU?
TC: Phew you better believe it.

I LOOKED IT UP AND YOUR LAST GAME WAS AS SUBSTITUTE AWAY AT BURNLEY.
TC: Yeah I got a good reception there, I always got a good reception there because I played there three years. I was a bit sorry to leave Middlesbrough but you get tw*ts like Malcolm who thinks that the club should be run by him. If there is anybody controversial then he just seems to want to get rid of them. Looking back on it, it was Malcolm Allison football club and not Middlesbrough football club and it was what he'd done and he'd achieved not the players. There was never any recognition for players and I thought that was wrong and he wasn't a good manager. He was a good coach I won't take that away from him but not a good manager, he couldn't talk to people he couldn't man manage.

MOONSTRUCK

My name is David Peacock (aka Deanos Doubles Cousin).
I'm originally from the Boro, but am currently living in Glasgow and spending far more than I can afford following them up and down the country.
The big 40 is coming up a bit too quickly, but it means that the period from the Stan Anderson years to the John Neal era are now permanantly clouded with a rose tinted hue.

THE FIRST GAME I think I remember is a game against Millwall in January 68, it may have been a cup game, but whatever, it ended up as a 2-2 draw. I went with my dad in the East End seats and vaguely remember big men in red shirts kicking a football about with big men in white shirts as well as two very scary skinny men in green shirts who spent all the time loitering against the goal posts smoking roll ups, although I may have made that bit up, not the scary bit though, Willie Whigham could still frighten the life out of me the last time I saw him about 10 years ago.

I HAVE TWO MOST MEMORABLE MOMENTS.
The first was the sheer ecstasy and joy of watching them win a semi-final of a Wembley Final cup competition for the first time. OK it was only ZDS, but it is my most frequently watched video and one of the few matches I can actually see when I close my eyes and dream. We may have been to some proper finals lately but we were a "big" team by then, not just 'The Boro'.

The second is for sheer imagery, our very own big friendly lion, stuffing a sly cheating wolf in a pre-match penalty competition. I just loved it as our size 35 bare pawed hero smashed goal after goal past a Nike wearing ner' do' well from the midlands. Never has an oversized cuddly toy punched the air with such passion and pride and got the crowd going as the wolf missed the target time after time, and they have the cheek to call half naked lasses pre match entertainment these days do they, no wonder nobody watches.

MY LOW MOMENT was when I refused to put any money in the door to door collecting buckets during that horrible time of administration. What a cheek I thought, all that gate money I'd given, all them bovrils bought, I still have the bloody Pheonix from the Flames badge to remind me that the only way was up (M. Allison), and after all that they were still going bust. Well I could live without them, I didn't care, they were always rubbish, there must be better things to do on a Saturday. Well of course I couldn't, I did, they weren't and there aren't. On the other hand where did all that money in the buckets end up?

COBBLERS TO THIS, I'M OFF FOR A KEBAB!
YOU REALLY DON'T GET IT DO YOU? THERE AREN'T ANY KEBAB SHOPS YET!
NO FOOTIE, NO BORO AND NOW NO KEBABS! YOU'VE BROUGHT US TO HELL!
I WOULDN'T MIND ONE OF THESE
WELL WHAT DO YA KNOW, THEY REALLY WERE BIGGER YEARS AGO!
MARS
IT'S A GOOD JOB GAZZA NEVER GOT LAMPED BY ONE OF THOSE!
BACK IN THE PRESENT
WHAT A CHUFFIN WASTE OF TIME THAT WAS!
ANYROAD, WE'RE HOME NOW AND WE'RE NOT USING THAT THING EVER AGAIN
AND JUST TO BE ON THE SAFE SIDE!
BACK IN THE STADIUM
ROOFUS, GET YOUR FLEA-BITTEN BUT IN MY OFFICE!
CHAIR
IT'S SO NICE TO BE BACK TO NORMAL!
COMING YOUR WORSHIPFULNESS!
I WANT THIS CLUB TO BE THE BEST IN EUROPE, AND IT'S NOT EASY WITH WASTERS LIKE YOU AND THOSE OTHER TWO HANGERS-ON!
AW BUT SIR JOHN, MAN!
AARGH
YOU STUPID PRATS, YOU'VE COCKED IT ALL UP. DAMN YOU ALL TO HELL!
IT'S CAUSE AND EFFECT - YOU'VE CHANGED EVERYTHING!
BUT SIR JOHN, YOU DON'T MEAN TOTALLY BIAS TOON BOY AND ALASTAIR SADMAN DO YA?
QUITE SIMPLY HADAWAY AND SHITE
TOON ARMY
IT'S ALL TOO MUCH FOR HIM - HE'S GONE CATATONIC!
WE'VE GOT TO GET BACK TO THE RIVER, FIND THE BATTERY AND PUT EVERYTHING BACK THE WAY IT SHOULD BE!
BACK AT THE RIVER
I THINK I MIGHT HAVE FOUND SOMETHING - EERR!
KEEP LOOKING SADMAN!
I'LL GIVE HIM ANOTHER HOUR OUT THERE THEN TELL HIM WE COULD ALWAYS GO AND BUY ONE FROM THE SHOP!
BACK AGAIN IN THE PRESENT?
WELL, I NEVER THOUGHT WE'D GET EVERYTHING BACK TO NORMAL!
AYE, IT TOOK A BIT OF DOING
FAT LOUIES KEBAB EMPORIUM
LARGE DONNER
CHICKEN SPECIAL
ALL'S WELL THAT ENDS WELL
IT'S JUST A GOOD JOB I HAD MY 'BORO BIBLE' WITH ME SO WE KNEW EXACTLY HOW EVERYTHING FITS INTO PLACE!
OCH, DO YA WANT CHILLI OR GARLIC ON THIS?
DOES HE LOOK FAMILIAR?
TRAINEE
NAAAR!

The FMTTM Millannual

fmttm's Xmas Ten of the Best

So, if you're reading this, it's probably just after Christmas dinner and you've got a mountain of gift vouchers to spend when the shops re-open (Around 16th January, these days). Here are a few ideas for ways to spend them down the Captain Cook's Centre, as the FMTTM book reviewer gives his ten of the best:

1/ Rothmans Football Yearbook 1999-2000
Published by Rothmans Headline,
Price £16.99

Statto Heaven. Details of just about every football team from Man United to Brache Sparta, major sections on all 92 teams in English Professional Football, including team photos. Every result in every major competition in England. Extensive coverage of Scottish, Irish, Welsh and European competitions. Useful for putting under extremely damaged table legs. OK, not such a bargain, halfway through the season, but still good value. You'll be boring your relatives with it long after New Years Day

2/ Survival of the Fattest 5
Published by Red Card,
Price £9.99

If you want truth about what sort of a season your team has had, read a fanzine. This is a collection of reviews of the season by the editors of all of the major English fanzines. Not quite all of the English teams are covered, but all the ones that count are. (Why haven't Barnsley got a fanzine? They can't still be in shock from two seasons ago). Quite interesting to read other teams' opinions of us (but not Arsenal, this year, which is a farrago of sub-Nick Hornby gloating. They only got 6, for god's sake).

3/ All Played Out
By Pete Davies, Published by Mandarin
Price £7.99

A better book about the England team has yet to be written. Davies had a roving remit to follow the England team through the 1990 World Cup Campaign, from the late qualifying stages to the famous meeting with West Germany in Rome. The insights on the team, players, manager and fans are eye opening. Amuse yourself by spotting all the bright young players who will end up in the Boro squad. Masterful.

4/ Tales From The Boot Camps
By Steve Claridge, Published by Vista
Price £5.99

I realise that this is probably a strange choice for a Boro fan, granted that Claridge scored the winning goal for Leicester against Boro in the Coco Pops Cup in 1997. Leicester is only a small part of the Claridge story - It's probably quicker to list the teams he didn't play for. An interesting take on a refreshingly eccentric player with a wide range of very human fallibility's. Also good for an insight into two of the maddest men to ever manage a football team, John Beck and Barry Fry. Remember, one Claridge is a better laugh than fifty Beckhams, and probably more fun at the betting shop too.

5/ Football Against the Enemy
By Simon Kuper, Published by Phoenix
Price £7.99

A personal favourite here. The sickeningly talented Kuper wrote this excellent survey of football fans around the world at the age of 23, before going into sports journalism for the Times. Basically, he toured the globe, watching football on every continent, from the gangsters who run Dynamo Kiev to the South African Kaizer Chiefs' personal witchdoctor. Strangely, the worst, most intolerant fans he found were the Old Firm in Scotland. Funny, isn't it, when they put on skirts and daft wigs, they become the darlings of world football support, instead of a bunch of hate-crazed shagnasties. The world, as Kuper proves, is strange when it comes to football.

6/ Where are they now?
By Andy Pringle and Neil Fissler, Published by Two Heads Price £9.99

Before Bosman and Player Power, you retired at 35 to 40 and got a proper job. Or a pub. This is a list of about 2000 players, mainly from the fifties, sixties and seventies, detailing what happened to them after they retired. A lot more fun than it sounds, finding, for instance, that Irving Nattrass now breeds horses and Willie Wigham frightens stray dogs in Motherwell. (Sorry, I lied about the last one). If I can level a criticism, however, Bosko, NOT Bozo, Jankovic, played for the Boro in the late 70's, before tragically being killed in Sarajevo in the Bosnian Crisis. RIP, Bosko.

The FMTTM Millannual

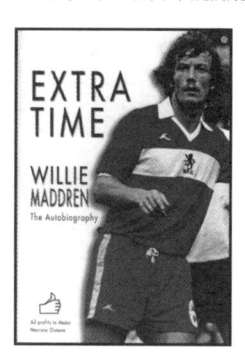

7/ Extra Time
By Willie Maddren, Published locally
Price £9.99

Not only a great book, written by a REAL Boro legend and loyal club servant for many years, but a chance to make somebody else's' Christmas happier, as all profits go to help the MND Society. This book, unlike so many footballers' autobiographies, is not ghostwritten, but told by Willie himself. A great account of a turbulent period in Boro's history, as well as Willie's truly heroic struggle against a crippling disease. Uplifting stuff from a brave man.

8/ My Favourite Year
Edited by Nick Hornby, Published by Gollancz
Price £5.99

A collection of short-story length accounts of the favourite seasons of different sportswriters, usually contributors to When Saturday Comes, who sponsored this book. Notable contributions include Middlesbrough 1991/92, from our own Harry Pearson and Booker Prizewinner Roddy Doyle's account of the Irish World Cup Campaign under Big Jack in 1990. My personal favourite is Olly Wicken's story of a year as a ballboy in Watford's 1974/75 demotion year, which is laugh-out-loud funny. Skip over Giles Smith, though (his best year was collecting Chelsea programmes without going to a single match, which says it all really), and Ed Horton (Oxford United, 1991/92) who should get off his soapbox and get out more.

9/ Parklife
By Nick Varley, Published by Micheal Joseph
Price £9.99

A truly brilliant book, taking in the changes that have come over English football in the last 10 years since the Hillsborough disaster. A view of a rapidly changing sport that informs without boring, generally using Leeds United as the model for how change has come to football. At the same time, Boro get frequent and sympathetic mention. The best part of the book, however, has to be the account of the Hillsborough Disaster, which is simply the best and clearest yet written.

10/ The Far Corner
By Harry Pearson, Published By Abacus
Price £6.99

THE book for the Boro supporter, by Boro's own writer. Harry spent the 1993/94 season touring the North-East, seeing games that took in the full spectrum from Boro to Evenwood Town (or should that be Newcastle United)? Funny? You bet. Particularly recommended for the 'Sunderland Skinheed' story ('He only hits tall blokes' 'but I'm six foot five!'). See also his comments on running around the kitchen in slow motion on hearing that Brian Robson has signed as manager of Boro. Probably the best footie book ever written. What more recommendation do you need?

Rob Hymer

RAV'S RANT
This millennium........The Roman and British Empires

You Eenglish - you kill me, you really do. You still go on about your piddly little empire. The British Empire. Ha! What was it - India and a few little islands in the southern hemisphere. What a joke! All you wanted was a hot country with lots of poor people who you could order about. And what has happened? You teach them your national game (cricket - don't get me started) and now they have independence and beat you easily at it. Just like at everything else, ha ha ha. But you crazy Eenglish still think there is a British Empire - look at your Commonwealth Games - I laugh so much my hat falls off. Ha ha ha. You have to win at something so you say I know, let's play those pesky Cook Islands at athletics, we are bound to win. You are so Sad, you Eenglish. You cling to what you think are former glories because you are so crap nowadays. And another thing - it must have taken a big effort to conquer the mighty Ascension Islands with their world-class military and huge army. Bollocks!

No, when it comes to Empires, we Italians can be proud. Our Roman ancestors conquered the world, even England. I bet our armies never went to Middlesburg though, even if it existed. But we ruled all the best places and we looked so good! Not like your Empire builders with their stupeed clothes and lack of headwear. No, our centurions were glamorous with their shiny helmets and their fetching tunics. If I wasn't such a hot-blooded Italian stallion, I would find them almost attractive. Even you Eenglish like them! Yes! You are fascinated by the way my forefathers built our homes in your land. And everywhere else. And we never bothered with the Cook Islands. We stuck to the vast continent of Europe and now, now we are not embarrassed about our past like you Eenglish. We are, how you say, proud as a pea in a pod. And our time will come again - yes, my friends, the Italians will once again rule the world, ha ha ha ha ha ha ha!

Fly Me To The Moon Productions proudly present

The Ravanelli Dolli

At last here it is - your chance to recreate Middlesbrough FC's almost glory days when cup finals were an everyday occurrence and relegation an impossibility with a squad of international superstars at the fingertips of master tactician Bryan Robson.

And no star was bigger or shone brighter (at least in the cups against lower division sides) than Fabrizio Ravanelli - the white feather, the silver fox, the idle showboating Italian!

In homage to those great days, FMTTM have commissioned a superb, hand crafted, limited edition replica of the whinging international, lovingly manufactured by world famous artist and Boro fan Stanley DeHavilland.

The beautiful Ravanelli Dolli has a host of features which will have you pining for the days of 6-0 and 7-0 victories in the cups and 1-0 defeats in the league.

- Super gripping hands to pull his shirt over his head in celebration.
- Hamstring panel which shows in extreme detail the snap which famously occurred after only 10 minutes of the FA Cup final.
- The Ravanelli Dolli is so realistic it even has no heart!

And that's not all, for the Ravanelli Dolli also speaks! Pull the cord and hear a variety of often heard Fabrizio phrases:

- Gol!
- I wanted always to play for Middlesbrough.
- Meeddlesbro industria filtha.
- I was misquoted
- OK then, I said it.
- Quick, get those light fittings before Lamby arrives!

Order within a fortnight and you can receive the Fabrizio Ravanelli accessory pack - absolutely free! The accessory pack contains sunglasses, a passport, an Italian journalist's phone number and a well-used suitcase.

Remember, The Ravanelli Dolli is a limited edition and is not available in the shops (yet). Order now to avoid disappointment!

NB The Ravanelli Dolli is guaranteed for 1 year only.

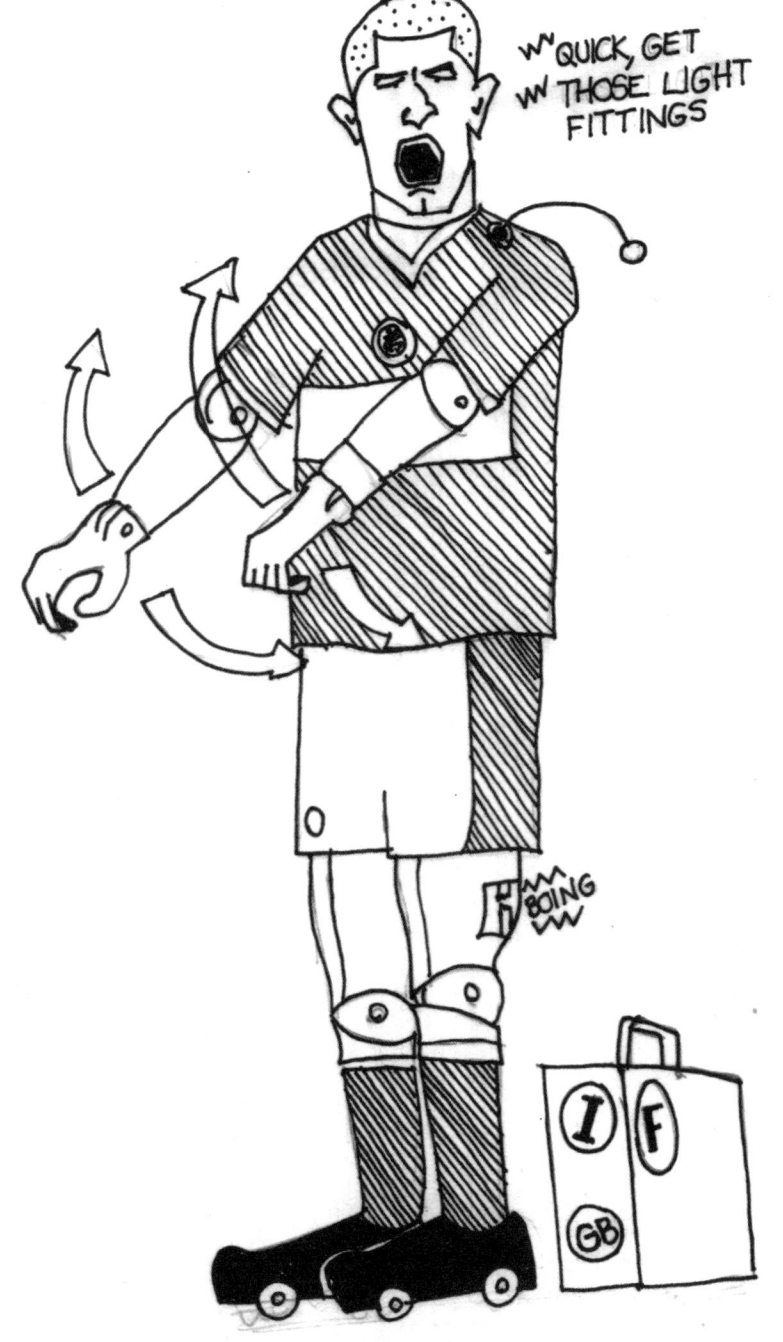

Stuart "Miniature G" Downing

… The FMTTM Millannual

The Gospel According to the Blessed Dave

Master Robbie Boal has an utterly charming Christmas-type story that has absolutely nothing to do with Middlesbrough or football whatsoever... what's it doing in here then? Err.. Dunno really. Never mind eh!

The prophet came to the village at the edge of the Red Sea. Although they were poor people the villagers recognised the prophet as being a man of God and so laid on some digs and a bit of nosh for him.

After a night's rest the prophet came to meet the men of the village - sorry girls but this was a couple of thousand years ago and you would not have been asked along to anything important. The men of the village, who were largely fishermen, told the prophet how despite they're being devout worshippers the fishing was poor and their lives were very difficult. They said that they were beginning to lose faith and that the bloke down the road had said he could knock them up a false idol for a couple of dozen mackerel and a bucketful of clams.

The prophet considered their problem and told them this parable:

Philip, of the Ehrick Hills, near Galilee, was experiencing great difficulties with his fishing. As a very young man he had shown himself to be an able apprentice and was always available to join crews if one of the more experienced members had to drop out on account of having had a "bad pint" the night before.

Since then however he had not lived up to the promise of his early years and younger men were being picked for crews ahead of him. He had great problems with his nets, if they were not too tangled for use they would be badly holed so that even when a chance to join a crew came up he would not be able to join due to his damaged twine. Then when his twine was in good repair and he was able to join a crew lack of recent fishing would see him undone. People of his village began to talk of deeper lying reasons for this than pure misfortune. Some claimed that although he went to the temple every morning he was not praying hard enough for him to have any success in the fleet.

Philip was praying as hard as he could though. He was just having a run of misfortune but even Philip himself could not see this. As his frustration grew he began to lose faith.

The leader of the fishermen could see this so decided to bolster Philip's faith. Against the wishes of many of the villagers he told Philip his share of the catch whether he was involved or not would increase. No matter what the state of Philip's faith the leader showed he had great faith in Philip.

Philip's luck began to change; all that praying was now paying off even if he looked like the least pious of the fishermen. He also showed his versatility by switching to a steering position at the back of the boat. These days he is even starting to get the grudging respect of his previously sternest critics in the village although Philip knows he must continue to give his all as they would relish the chance to have another pop at him.

The men of the Village decided to sleep on the meaning of this parable. Having done so the next morning they engaged in a bit of arse kicking upon the prophet, encouraging him to leave and never return. They thought the parable of poor Philip a very meaningful tale but could not see what it had to do with their predicament. The bloke down the road was duly paid his mackerel and clams. The villagers were now able to praise and cavort around baked goat dung fashioned into the shape of a smirking halibut. Fishing had never been better!

**THIS IS THE WORD OF DAVE
PRAISE BE TO DAVE**

ROBBIE BOAL

RAV'S RANT

This millennium . . . . Millennium Eve

I am glad I am still not at Middlesburg. I would have to spend the Millennium Eve in your silly little Heathen country. All you Eenglish are bothered about is how much it will cost you to go out and, how you say, boogie on down. You make me sick, you Eenglish. In case you hadn't noticed, it will be the 2000th anniversary of the birth of our lord Jesus. Us Italians like any good Catholic country will celebrate the Millennium with prayers, thanksgivings and perhaps half a glass of Chianti. You Eenglish, you will just go and get pissed as a lizard or whatever it is you say. You will say to your friends, remember the Millennium Eve, I had such a good time, I nearly died of alcoholic poisoning. Ha! You have no idea. And that big wheel - what is that all about? If you were good Catholics you would feel so guilty about it that you would all be saying Hail Marys for the rest of the year. No wonder the bloody French copied it, you are as bad as each other with your heathen ways. And as for the Millennium Dome, well . . . . . .

The FMTTM Millannual

JIM PLATT (1970s)
Platty played in Big Jack's team,
Back in the seventies,
He'd catch the ball and stop the shots,
And even penalties.

THE SECRET DIARY OF CRAIG SUMMERDALE AGED 20 AND A QUARTER

FRIDAY 17TH DECEMBER 1999

Well, frankly dear diary, things are at breaking point - and for once I don't mean the elastic on Mr Stamp's shorts. I have finally decided that here in Middlesbrough my career is not moving at the pace it really should be and so today I stormed into Mr Robson's office to demand a showdown.

"I want a transfer and I want one NOW!!!" I shouted, slamming my fist down quite hard (ouch!) on Mr Robson's desk.

"You can't have one," he replied. "You'll have to make do with a sticker book like all the rest of the juniors." I felt a bit guilty almost straight away, it was obvious that Mr Robson was really busy this afternoon, what with Jerry Springer being on and then Childrens ITV starting at a quarter-past-three.

"No, really!" I insisted. "I feel I'm not being allowed to make the first-team breakthrough that I deserve and with opportunities here at Middlesbrough being so limited I've decided the best thing for all concerned would be for me to look for another club..."

I looked up to find Mr Robson staring at me even more wide-eyed and open-mouthed than usual. Clearly I had impressed him with my impassioned speech (in fact taken from Chapter 7 of "How to Talk like a Professional Footballer" by Dr. N. Webb of Reading University) and I had caught him very much on the wrong foot. However once I stepped off it (According to that nice Bob Ward, Mr Robson is a martyr to his bunions) he started to calm down a little and walked around the desk to put a comforting arm around my shoulder.

"Now listen Andy" he said to me, softly, "You've got to believe me when I say I think you're one of the best young strikers in the country..."

"But my name's Craig," I replied. "And actually I'm a sort of attacking midfielder who can also play at right-back when Mr Geddis feels there's a left-winger up against us who's particularly hopeless..."

"Whatever," he replied. "But Middlesbrough is a progressive club. Everbody here is determined to move forward as quickly as possible, and believe me, we're all part of a huge family effort, you as much as anybody. And if at any point you should doubt the seriousness of our ambitions, I would say - take a look at these magnificent training facilities..." And at that point he pulled open the blinds on his window to reveal the lovely rolling fields of Rockliffe Park, bang in the middle of which was a wobbly-looking Mr Gascoigne dressed in a French Maids outfit and driving a tractor while shooting at passing starlings with a large pump-action water pistol. Mr Robson hastily closed the blinds again.

"...what you have to bear in mind is sometimes in football you have to look to the short-term as well as the long-term. And so, Anthony - "

" Craig," I corrected him.

"Whatever... it's sometimes necessary for me to nuture the stars of the future such as yourself for a little while longer while I concentrate on shelling out untold millions of pounds for slightly over-the-hill ex-Internationals in their thirties. Do you understand, Mark?"

"Y-e-e-e-e-s...." I replied.

"But believe you me, the money here at Middlesbrough is NOT a bottomless pit. No, that's in the gym where Mr Stamp jumped off the vaulting horse and went straight through the floorboards. And one day, I promise, your time will come. After all, young talents like yourself are the future of this club. And we have to rely on people like you because unfortunately we just don't have the finance to be able to compete with the likes of Arsenal and Chelsea..."

And with that he put his arm so far around me that it almost felt as if his hand was inside my jacket. I wiped a tear from my eye, nodded and picked up my transfer request with no small degree of shame. How could I have doubted the club's sincerity? Its ambition? Its ruthless drive for success? I left without a word.

It was only when I got outside that I realised that my wallet was missing from my inside jacket pocket. I toyed with the idea of going back in the office to ask Mr Robson if he'd seen it but when I listened at the door I could hear that he was rather busy again. He seemed to be counting, and was muttering something like "One hundred and forty... one hundred and fifty... one hundred and sixty! I'm obviously paying these young lads too much money, still thanks Jason, that should do for Incey's gas bill for a month. Now, I wonder if Stevie Baker's unsettled too?"

But then again I could be mistaken. Right then! Back to the normal life of a young and promising Boro reserve star. I have to clean the North Stand with a toothbrush before seven o'clock...

Love, Craig xxx

G-R-E-A-T BORO MOMENTS

STUART BOAM

*"6ft 2 - Eyes of blue
Stuart Boam is after you."*

The captain fantastic of the all-conquering Charlton's Champions.
He took no prisoners on the pitch. Strikers quaked in their boots when Boamy gave them his calling card tap around the ankles.
Strong, powerful and forged the greatest ever Boro defensive partnership with Willie Maddren. A ROCK.

Players in the Moon — GARY HAMILTON

FIRST GAME
My first game was against Barnsley away. The reason I was on the bench was that Joe Bolton was injured and I had played some games at left back in the reserves so I got on with thirty minutes left, we lost 2-1. I think the winner was my fault as the winger got past me, made a cross and scored in the last five mins. So that was not the best start but I did enjoy it some how. I had just turned seventeen.

BEST MEMORY
My best memories of my time at the Boro, well there were so many, but it has to be the Rioch era, they were the best. It was a good team with a tremendous bunch of lads who just wanted to do well for the town plus we were shit scared of Bruce at the beginning but no matter what anybody say's he wanted us all to do well also.

BEST PERFORMANCE
My best performance, everybody and their grandmother thinks it's the Bradford game (play off) but in my own eyes it was when we played Leeds at home in '85 and it was 0-0. It's the first time that I got any ten out of tens in the papers. That's the best game I played, hopefully I didn't do too bad in a lot of others.

LAST GAME
My last game for the Boro was against Sheffield Wed 1989 last game of the season that sent us down. To be honest I should have never played that game or many others that season, reasons not to mention. I put in that much work into trying to get back my wife nearly left me. All I wanted to do was play again and I was not going to accept anything less no matter what they were telling me. Then one day after putting my family through hell and back, as I was not the most reasonable person to be around at that time, and after the knee was not responding to the work load that I needed to do it was time to make a decision. It was hard but people make a lot harder decisions every other day.

future imperfect

Ian Cusack writes of the disturbing trends that could lead to football's Armageddon

As we reach the end of the millennium, it seems compulsory in all fields of human endeavour to take stock of the changes and achievements of the past thousand years. In football terms this is not a helpful chronology as, on the eve of the second millennium, we were in the dark ages and not just because of a lack of floodlights. On January 1st 1000, using the old Julian Calendar, it was still some 855 years before the formation of the world's oldest club, Sheffield FC and 863 years before the founding of the Football Association. No, for football fans it is instructive to look back a mere 100 years.

On 1st January 1900, Aston Villa were the reigning champions of an 18 team top division, having held off the challenges of Liverpool and Sunderland. Second division champions The Wednesday (Sounds like a 60s psychedelic beat group to me) and runners-up Bolton Wanderers had displaced Burnley and Glossop North End, the latter now playing in the North West Trains League, in the top flight. Sheffield United prevailed in the FA Cup final 3-1 at Crystal Palace over Derby County. Middlesbrough made their debut in the football league, losing 3-0 away to Lincoln City and Newcastle finished 5th in their second season in the top flight, winning 2-1 away at Roker Park on the last day of the season. Victoria was on the throne, the Boer War raged and five years before Alf Common's £1,000 move, transfer fees remained in three figures. Footballers were little more than serfs in the employ of despotic chairman.

Despite changing personnel on the throne and more global conflicts, football remained essentially the same for 60 years, off the pitch that is. Floodlights, European football, the mighty Magyars and the Revie Plan may have refined the way the game was played, but boardroom tyrants still regarded players as little more than domestic servants. The maximum wage was still in place, Charlie Mitten was barred for life after seeking his fortune in Colombia and Tom Finney was told by a Preston director to concentrate on his plumbing business rather than seek a move to Serie A. Then, in Summer 1960, the first rays of the twentieth century shone across football. George Eastham had asked for a transfer from Newcastle. The board turned it down, so he asked again. This time they not only refused, they effectively put his career in limbo, years before Jean Marc Bosman suffered a similar fate, by retaining his registration, but refusing to play or pay him, as they were then entitled to. Eastham took his case to the High Court on the grounds of restraint of trade, won and moved to Arsenal. Perhaps Stockton lad Harold McMillan was referring to footballers' rights when he uttered his famous "You've never had it so good" speech.

Eastham's landmark judgement, whilst unfortunately popularising Jimmy Hill as head of the PFA, together with the abolition of the maximum wage in 1962, saw the beginnings of the juggernaut of player power, currently travelling at the speed of light. Indirectly those two decisions, made almost 40 years ago, were responsible for the Hasselbaink and Anelka situations of Summer 1999. George Best apart, the swinging sixties did not impinge too much on football. England's World Cup win and the twin European successes of Celtic and Manchester United owed more to Harold Wilson than Haight Astbury, though England's capitulation to West Germany in the Mexico World Cup did have the whiff of a sporting Altamont about it.

Off the pitch, the game was evolving slowly. Freedom of contract and foreign players may have arrived in the late 1970s, though the game was in steep decline by then. Greedy chairmen had reaped the rewards of a post World Cup boom in attendances, but had done little or nothing to arrest the subsequent haemorrhaging of support once hooliganism began to take a grip. Or is that is a simplistic view? Perhaps crowds tailed off because arrogant, short sighted businessmen, with a greater love for profit margins than the game itself, refused to make stadia comfortable places to watch football and as a result saw their consumer base almost halve. Whatever the root cause, the inescapable fact remains that attendances fell from a high of 30,107,298 in 1969-1970 to 16,488,577 in 1985-1986, the year after Bradford, Heysel and the Millwall riot at Luton. This figure seems unbelievable as money at the gate was, even allowing for the relatively recent innovation of shirt sponsorship, until the advent of Sky TV, by far the biggest single contributor to football's income. Nowadays, with total crowds just over the 25 million mark for 1998-1999, the fact that this is less than the aggregate for the 1977-1978 season is immaterial. Back then people weren't paying £40 for a replica shirt and £30 a month to Rupert Murdoch.

The low water mark was reached at the end of the 1980s. Margaret Thatcher, an avowed and implacable enemy of the working class, hated football. Her policies, as carried out by the loathsome Colin Moynihan and backed up by fascistic Chief Constables, still fired up on testosterone and a lavish Miners' Strike overtime bonus funded lifestyle, criminalized the average football fan. Not just the yobbo element either. Ordinary, peaceful match going types like us were treat like vermin. Sure there were abortive campaigns against her identity card scheme, but the inescapable feeling was, in the police state that 1980s Britain had become, she would get her way. Tragically, it took the deaths of 96 innocent Liverpool fans, caught up in a tragic ▶

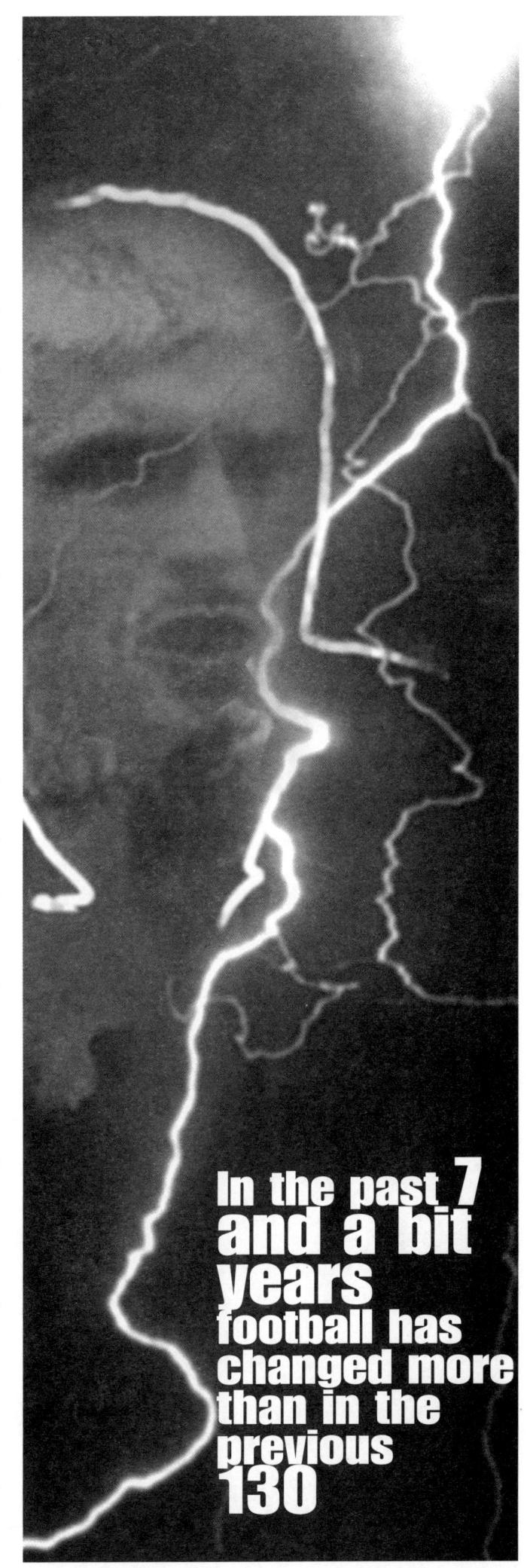

In the past 7 and a bit years football has changed more than in the previous 130

cocktail of police brutality and football authority indifference, to finally drag football into the twentieth century. Sure new football grounds aren't as atmospheric as they used to be, but people won't die in them in future.

Amazingly, just over a year after Hillsborough, football was trendy again. Thatcher and Moynihan were gone, replaced by John Major, who admittedly was a bona fide football fan, and Italia 90 had redrawn the sporting demographic map. Not since The Malvinas War had English people been united in a single cause. The E generation were donning replica shirts and going to the match. Club chairmen, in an unprecedented show of foresight, stoked the boilers of the best gravy train yet and plonked their ample buttocks down in first class. Corporate jargon entered the boardroom; football became a commodity, we were consumers, "quality" was compulsory. Top-flight clubs, then including Luton, Notts County and Oldham, decided in Summer 1991, they wanted a super league. Their rhetoric may have alluded to an increase in playing standards, but truthfully they just wanted a bigger share of whatever money there was sloshing about. Little did they know how much money was about to come their way. The Taylor Report had condemned huge swathes of terracing and dozens of stands, rendering many grounds unviable for further development. The money for new ones had to come from somewhere. Despite a donation from the Government in the shape of a reduction in the football pools levy, a shortfall was obvious. Then came Rupert Murdoch, riding in on his white charger, his saddlebags stuffed with used fivers, promising unimaginable wealth. Joseph Conrad described the stampede to exploit mineral resources in the Belgian Congo at the end of the nineteenth century as "the vilest scramble for loot that everdisfigured the human conscience". He could have been talking about the establishment of the Premier League.

Of course the scabby old Football League Division One title was jettisoned and the FA Carling Premiership marque was adopted. At first this meant going to grounds that had only three sides open (Remember the Arsenal mural?), or skinning your knees every time you moved, as seats were bolted onto terracing. Yet, the Sky TV hype kept the whole thing moving. The inspired choice of Andy Gray as chief analyst, fantastic camera work and the regular marrying of popular culture, by means of music or television personalities being linked with clubs, made following a team the easiest thing in the world. Especially when Graham Taylor was managing to turn the England side into the laughing stock of the world, a job now in the capable hands of old Baseball Bat himself.

In the past seven and a bit years football has changed more than in the previous one hundred and thirty. For fans, both diehard and armchair, for players and especially for the enormous mass of media and corporate camp followers. In the north east, supporters of the big three attend home games not in ramshackle fleapits, last painted for the 66 World Cup, but in state of the art sporting palaces, watching fabulously well paid international superstars, and Phil Stamp. Even Darlo and Hartlepool fans find their surroundings far superior. Though at £11 a shot for Third Division football, you'd expect things to have improved. Even though gate money is a minor source of income at the highest echelons of the game, it hasn't stopped my season ticket going up from £130 to almost £500 in less than a decade. Though there is the inescapable sense that supporters are no longer important to the game itself. Indeed, nouveau riche Chairmen who took over from the Bob Lord era local potentates are now being outmanoeuvred. The players and their agents now hold all the aces and the only way to complete is to be owned by a multinational conglomerate with immense spending power.

For the first few years of the Sky deal, Premiership chairmen, like European imperial rulers in the early days of the worldwide growth of Capitalism, felt that nothing could go wrong. A TV deal poured huge amounts in to the coffers, all of which was profit now grounds were up to scratch. Merchandising sales

The atrocious arrogance as displayed by Hasselbaink, Hamann and especially Anelka proves that contracts are no longer worth the paper they are written on

tune in drop out

Given Sky TV's influence upon the game, it is surely no accident that, post 1992, with the greater exposure given to Manchester United than to Liverpool, in comparison to the latter's similar period of success in the 1970s and 1980s, a more penetrative marketing reach has been achieved by the team from Old Trafford than the Anfield Road side ever could have hoped for. Recent surveys suggest up to 20% of the population of England support Manchester United. Sky TV has helped bring this about, almost by accident. Imagine what their potential could have been, if the DTI had not blocked their Old Trafford buy out plans.

went through the roof. Then the name of Bosman became the spectre to haunt Europe. At first it didn't matter that a few players allowed their contracts to lapse and move on. Leeds didn't suffer unduly when Rod Wallace moved on. Newcastle fans smirked at Darren Peacock leading Blackburn to relegation. Of course there was the odd player, Ravanelli and Emerson for example, who could act up, but that was just temperament, nothing widespread or infectious. Even van Hoojidonk's extended summer holiday was regarded as arrogance and not as a sinister development. It seemed to the Chairmen that, if everyone else was tied nice and tight on long term deals, the license to print money would continue. Golden hellos, annual salary reviews that sort of thing, they'd keep the players quiet. Then agents, real hard nosed money grabbers, not pantomime villains like Eric Hall, got involved.

The atrocious arrogance as displayed by Hasselbaink, Hamann and especially Anelka proves that contracts are no longer worth the paper they are written on. Hamann had four years on his deal, Hasselbaink three, yet such was the destabilising influence of their actions on dressing rooms, transfers were seen as the only solution. Yet, lest anyone fool themselves that their actions are just the product of a foreign temperament, there was the case of Francis Jeffers. Less than 20 first team games and a handful of goals and this lifelong Evertonian wanted a move before he was old enough to vote!! The future looks bleak. Players will move from club to club each summer, seeking bigger signing on fees and ever more ludicrous wages and stalwart players like Mustoe or Howey or Kevin Ball will be as anachronistic as crush barriers or Pukka Pies.

So what of the future? There will be a slump, eventually. Of that there can be no doubt. Only the very strong of the very perceptive will survive. In the 1960s, a bunch of businessmen, Tiny Rowland, Jim Slater, James Goldsmith and Mohammed Al Fayed became famous as asset strippers. The bought up companies and conglomerates, separated off the various sectors of the business, closed down the unprofitable sections and made a killing by selling on the rest. Ted Heath called it "the unacceptable face of capitalism". For years, until Margaret Hilda's share owning democracy became a reality, this lot continued on their merry way, making unimaginable fortunes, untouched by the vicissitudes of the boom and slump economy. However, the new capitalist world order changed them forever. They became irrelevancies; dinosaurs. Rich as Croesus, but dinosaurs all the same. Slater fills in his days obsessively playing Monopoly, Rowland died a broken man, unable to adapt and Goldsmith is also dead, filling his last years with a fug of conspiracy theories that resulted in him forming the ill-judged Referendum Party. Al Fayed is alive and well, sharing his energies between Fulham and Harrods. In a way, he must be a kind of role model for football chairmen everywhere. He has learned to adapt. In the post Bosman era, clubs can not carry on attempting to make huge piles of money, regardless of what pay per view and the next Sky deal has in store, they must be aware that, for the moment, they are no longer dark satanic mills exploiting players on the treadmill of football. Clubs are now flowers, susceptible to bad weather and pounding footsteps, impotently hoping for pollenation by the free spirited bees that are players.

One hundred years ago they had two divisions and 36 senior clubs. What price a return to that? With rumoured mergers between Oldham, Bury and Rochdale and Wimbledon and Palace, surely the FA and Football League will repeal the law that says merged clubs must takeover the lowest league position of the teams involved. With Portsmouth, Chester, Luton, Mansfield and Palace teetering on the verge of extinction, the greatest surprise is that, since Accrington Stanley called it a day in 1962, only two other teams, Maidstone and Aldershot, have gone to the wall. The League Cup will die and the FA Cup, cruelly undermined by the ludicrous new third round date and Manchester United's withdrawal, may be on the slippery slope to debasement. Whatever happens, the game is no longer under the control of the authorities.

The Free Market, ten years after Thatcher was consigned to the dustbin of history, is rampant in football. Just as Gordon Brown's first act as Chancellor was to devolve the power to set the base rate to the Bank of England, thus effectively saying the market was beyond Government regulation, so the FA's encouragement of Manchester United to skip this season's Cup shows that ▶

no longer can we expect to see a unifying or unified body looking after football in this country. Manchester United, Chelsea and Arsenal will sail on, unimaginably rich through merchandising deals and multinational investments, purveyors of superb football because of great coaches. Soon they'll be out of sight for the rest of us. A second tier of Liverpool, Villa, Newcastle, Spurs and Leeds will emerge, under the wing of other multinational business empires followed by Everton, Boro, The Mackems and perhaps Blackburn, either hoping for a takeover or limping behind as they are still owned by Chairmen. The owners may be fantastically rich compared to the likes of us, but are of minimal influence to the global economy. For the rest, merger or bankruptcy will be a way of life.

Yet, whatever happens, we'll still be there and, such is the power that personal ties with clubs have, those five million armchair supporters of Manchester United will also still be there. Our strength, such as it is, is tradition.

Ian Cusack

Marooned on Moon Island — Adrian Bevington, The F.A.

FIVE MATCH VIDEOS
1. Boro 2 Everton 2 FA Cup 4th Round replay 1988
2. Boro 3 Liverpool 3 FA Premier League 1996
3. Boro 4 Arsenal 1 FA Cup 1977
4. Boro 4 Tottenham 1 1st Division 1980
5. Boro 3 Chesterfield 3 FA Cup 1997

MEMORABILIA
My Dad's and my own collection of Boro programmes, dating back to the 1940s and the Gazette's "Boro's Going Up" Special from 1967. Also my ticket stubs from the Carlisle game in the Full Members Cup 1985 (lowest crowd) and my Wembley tickets stubs - I felt I'd earned them.

BORO PERSON
Jack Charlton, Big Mal and Robbo would be a recipe for an almighty hangover! But who could resist? Also Jack could help catch our tea!

FIRST MATCH
Boro 3 Mansfield 0 Anglo Scottish Cup 1975. I was sat in the East End (Linthorpe Road End) of Ayresome. My earliest memory is of the crowd at the Holgate End chanting *"Fatty, Fatty Foggon, Fatty, Fatty Foggon"* and the smell of stale pipe tobacco - I was so excited I loved it!

BEST MEMORY
Ravanelli's goal going in at Derby in the FA Cup 6th round. I knew we'd broken the jinx - everyone began hugging one another in such delight at The Baseball Ground. Boro were so unusually professional that day, after their historical mishaps. The crowd on the way out began the chant *"Tell your Mam to put the champagne on ice - We're going to Wembley twice!!!"*

WORST MEMORY
Without doubt relegation against Leeds - tears for souvenirs that day. Chelsea's first goal in the FA Cup Final a week later didn't make me feel too good either.

G-R-E-A-T BORO MOMENTS

Hickton penalty - he's coming home... he's coming home

The FMTTM Millannual

The FMTTM Millannual

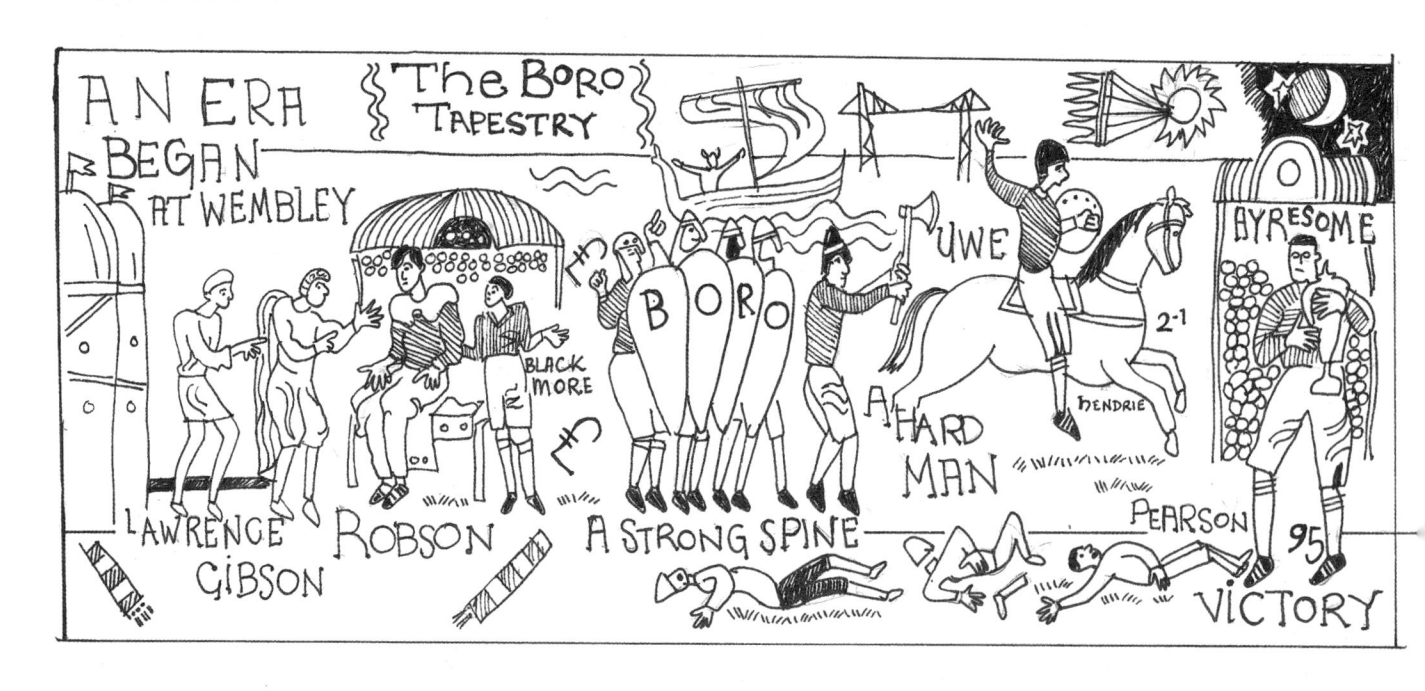

I Confess....

KEVIN KEEGAN, CHARLIE AMER AND ME....

Fly Me To The Moon's backroom boys enter the confessional and hang their heads in shame as they finally come clean and admit to the sins that have haunted them since their misspent and callow youths.

They throw themselves at the mercy of our specially convened kangeroo court, where there is no mercy only cries of hang'em, flog 'em and then send their battered and bruised remains off for transportation to some far flung colony like...err Hull. Yes, so you call yourself Middlesbrough fans do you? Ha... we shall see about that. Step forward please **Chris Bartley** of Normanby Top and present your case to the good people ofpeople of the Fly Me jury.

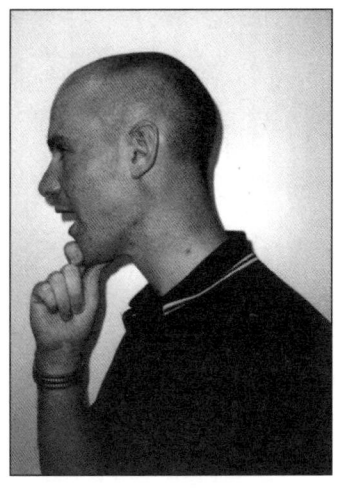

In my formative years as a football fan in the early 70's, there were two genuine, bona fide superstar footballers in this country. George Best was one but he was already in freefall at this stage and at South Eston Junior School, he was already a figure of fun. At many playtimes, we would chant mantra-like, 'GEORGIE BEST SUPERSTAR, HE WEARS FRILLY KNICKERS AND HE WEARS A BRA'. Kevin Keegan was the other superstar but he wouldn't be caught hanging around with models and drinking in night-clubs. He was a salt of the earth type bloke. He had a steady girlfriend called Jean who he married and the values taught by his Dad who was a miner, seemed to ensure that he has never done too many foolish things, barring the infamous perm fiasco of 1977. So when I found out that he was opening the 1973 summer fete in the palatial grounds of Normanby Hall, I pleaded with my Dad to take me.

In the 70's, footballers didn't quite have the kudos they have now. No invites to movie premieres or blind dates with pop stars were bandied about then. In the 70's, footballers were reduced to the celebrity B-list activities of opening supermarkets or opening garden fetes.

So the Bartley family went en masse to the fete and I think I took a white blank sealed envelope if the chance arose of procuring his autograph. It was a balmy summer day, classic English garden fete weather and it was the one day in every year that Chairman Charlie allowed the good people of Normanby to engage in the noble pursuits of hoopla, bingo and tombola. The stalls however were the sideshow. Everyone was here to see Kev, fresh from his recent UEFA Cup triumph against Borussia Munchen-hardtospellifyouwereonlynineatthetime. The car pulled up on the epic drive of Normanby Hall. It was probably a Merc or a BMW but I've never been a kid who knows about cars and my concern was observing the movements of Keegan so I could make a move with a military like precision and get that all important signature. My chances looked grim as Charlie and several other be-suited blokes went to greet him as he stepped out of the car. The next bit is a blur. I don't know whether I was pushed forward by me mam or whether I got a head of steam and went for it but inexplicably I found

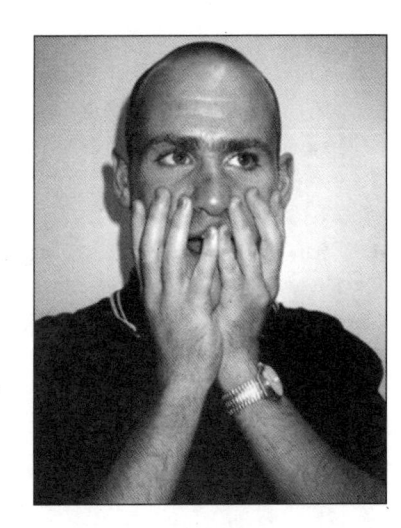

75

myself running for Kevin Keegan. Charlie and the boys tried to usher him into the lobby of Normanby Hall and it looked grim for the wee lad from Normanby but at the very moment when I stopped in my tracks, feeling a tad embarrassed, KK caught a glance out of the corner of his eye of a rather sheepish looking young lad clutching pen and blank sealed envelope and he broke away from the entourage and walked down the driveaway and signed an autograph. What a decent bloke I thought to myself. He made my day and there was no denying it. It was a truly magnanimous gesture and he was a God in front of very eyes.

When he became both a player and manager for Newcastle, I had to hate him of course because geography decrees that thou shalt hate any team or player of that team within a fifty mile radius of your home club but I did used to feel a bit guilty about it baring in mind the kindness he showed that day in 73. At least now he is England manager, we have reconciled again and I can feel there is a patriotic bond between us. Kevin Keegan, what a top fella.

Chris Bartley

JUDGEMENT: Stand up Christopher Bartley for you have committed a sin against the family of Middlesbrough. At a time when you should have been hanging off Big Jack's fishing tackle you were instead hanging off the bronzed and bullworkered arm of Kevin Keegan.

In your defence Special K is now the manager of our nationhood and it is also true that he did represent the country on Superstars. But taking all things into consideration I feel that I can only come to one conclusion. Chris Bartley you are guilty of a crime against Boro humanity and therefore I must recommend (with relish) that you are taken henceforth from this place and forced to wear a ridiculous curly perm and banish the letter "h" from your vocabulary forever.

This is however only a recommendation and it is up to you good, kind, decent people of the jury to decide which way the scales of justice will swing. Swing 'em high.

I Confess.....

By Simon "The Wanderer" Bolton

It is before God and the massed ranks of Boro faithful that I must confess of a terrible childhood affliction. Before I saw the light and started worshipping at the goodly Ayresome Park, I did wander a devilish path that led me to a most unholy place. That place was the very essence of evil for it did entrap me in its satanic snare and turn me truly to the dark side. Friends, fellow worshippers at the Temple Of St Bryan, I confess that, in the dark days of my youth, I was a Liverpool fan and it was at Anfield that I gave myself to Beelzebub himself - yes, I did worship Kenny Dalglish.

(A few moments of silent contemplation)

Oh come on, it's not that bad, I was only ten years old at the time, no one in my family supported Boro and Liverpool were on the telly all the time plus they were winning everything in sight, I mean what was I to do? I did jack it all in by the time I was ten and turned back to the good side so surely I can be forgiven. As it happens I did have the curly perm at the time but thankfully no ridiculous tash or garish shell suit, nor the urge to nick every set of hubcaps I set my eyes on, so I wasn't a true adopted scouser. I think I should get away with only a small penance - surely giving up following the Liverpool team of the eighties to support the Boro of the early eighties was penance enough!

Judgement: That's what you think is it Mr Bolton, or should that be Simon Liverpool from now on. I think so. How could you possibly even consider comparing the likes of Dalglish, Rush, Clemence and Hansen with the wonders and delights of Mick Saxby, Pat Heard, Kelham O'Hanlon and Bobby Thomson? I'm sorry but quite frankly it just doesn't wash. If it were only in my powers I would pronounce you very, very guilty indeed. The Terry Mc moustache and Phil Thompson beak combination mask kit is in the post. Wear it with pride at the next Supporters Club evening.

I Confess.....

Please step forward
Mr Robert Patrick Fischer of Kirklevington

Every Boro fan can remember it - the proud and poignant moment of your first ever match. Mine - aged 8 years old - was against Nottingham Forest on the 10th October 1981, and I could barely sleep the night before just thinking about the prospect of seeing all my footballing heroes stepping out onto that famous Ayresome Park turf. Unfortunately at the time my footballing heroes were (don't laugh) Peter Shilton, Garry Birtles, Trevor Francis, Larry Lloyd and Bryn Gunn. Yes, I admit it - I was a Forest fan. A couple of years of European Glory and the enduring charisma of Brian Clough had turned half my school into rabid Forestophiles, even if most of us had no idea where Nottingham actually WAS, let alone any prospect of ever getting to their matches. So this was the pinnacle of achievement for me, and the fact that Bryn Gunn scored an own goal early in the second half to make the final score 1-1 took none of the shine off the occasion at all. "Brian Clough can walk on water!!!" I chanted over and over again at school that week, pointing a tiny eight-year-old finger at sundry knee-high Liverpool fans. I was a Tricky Tree to the core, the City Ground (wherever it was) was my spiritual home, and my unbending, lifelong devotion to Cloughie and the boys was surely as unyielding as the ocean, as perennial as the grass. Until, that is, I went to my second Boro match five weeks later and saw Billy Ashcroft score twice in the last fifteen minutes of a ripping 3-3 draw against Aston Villa. "Trevor Francis?" I asked my Dad on the way home, "Who's he?" - and I've never looked back since. Big Billy was the business, and the Boro were my team from now on. But for that early, Forest-fancying fling, I throw myself on the mercy of the court. Sorry.

Judgement: K'yeah right, as your very own Donkeywatch column would most probably proclaim. Mercy is it, mercy you've got to be joshing son. What kind of excuse is this? ".... Half my school were rabid Forestophiles." Right Oh! Where was that school, Herr Fischer, in fair Nottingham County perhaps? Or was it slightly further afield in Arnold sadmad Township nought but a mere arrow head's distance away from the Sherriff of Nottingham's place?

Or was that supposed hotbed of East Midlands mayhem in fact slightly closer to home. Perhpas somewhere in that bastion of all things outlawry and Lincoln Green, like the badlands of Yarm? Tricky Trees, Tall Trees more like...

Guilty... Guilty.. Guilty.

Forest forfeit - you shall be taken to a changing-room some miles hence from this place but close by the lulling waters of the River Trent and thereupon you shall be forced to endure the enrapturing team talk of that inspirational leader of men they call David Platt. Enjoy!

The Way They Were

Young Mark in anorak and tie combination shocker.

Chairman Colin Henderson comments on Boro's new signing, "Mark's brimful of potential and has all the agility and flexibility we need to take this club forward... Lamby will fix you up with the brush and you can start on the Boardroom chimney straight away."

Mark Summerbell

I Confess....

It's a funny thing really but I can remember quite clearly my brother Stephen's first game at Ayresome Park but I haven't a clue what mine was.

I wasn't even there, but I know that my younger brother beat me to the hallowed turf at Ayresome. He was six years old when our dad took him along on a freezing cold Saturday in January to watch Eric McMordie, Georgie Smith, Joe Laidlaw and the great penalty gunslinger himself John Hickton shoot down York City in the FA Cup 4th Round. In case you haven't got a Glasper handy that was the January of 1970. Anyway the only reason for me mentioning this strange differential memory loss is to illustrate the fact that I wasn't a massive football fan as a kid. In fact I remember when all the lads from our street would discuss what they wanted to be when they grew up they all replied with the number shirt they wanted to wear for Middlesbrough. As for me I said I wanted to be a lorry driver, or more specifically a petrol tanker driver. Which just about summed it all up really. Which is by way of leading up to a whopping great excuse for the most heinous of juvenile crimes. When I was a bairn I used to not only support Scotland but worse, far, far worse then that I took a passing fancy to a team in stripes... no I can't say it.... Gulp, OK. Ready or not, here goes. I was partial to Newcastle United.

I cut out a picture of Newcastle from the Tiger comic with names like John Tudor, Stuart Barraclough and Malcolm Macdonald. Macdonald was my favourite and I had a picture of him on my bedroom wall. Not the infamous one where his tackle has spilled forth, but a head and shoulders shot of Super Mac in bristling burner overkill.

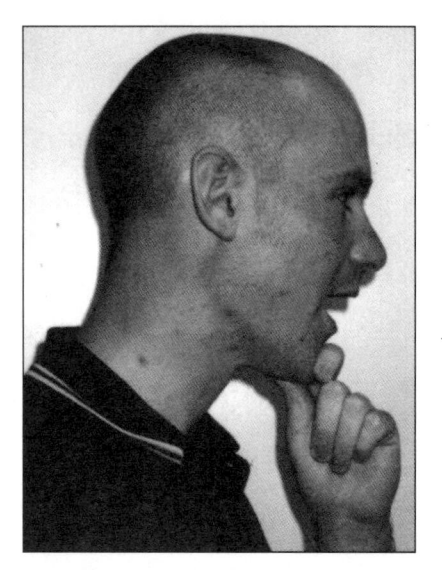

Unfortunately there's worse to come, because my sensible brother and me saved up tokens from Tudor crisp packets, he sent for a plastic Middlesbrough rosette badge and I sent for a plastic Newcastle one.

It's a terrible admission I know but at least I never went to a Newcastle game, my passion didn't extend beyond an occasional Sunday afternoon Shoot. And thankfully it didn't take me long to see the light. In half the time it took Sir Alfred McAlpine to convert the building site at St James' into a new stand I was back in the Boro camp.

John Hickton replaced MacDonald and Newcastle and petrol tankers were most definitely consigned to the rubbish bin of the past. I have been in denial about this unfortunate episode ever since but they say it is good to air things in public and confide to a friend. Yet in my limited experience talking about a problem only ever seems to make matters worse. I can only plead for mercy and ask that your judgement will not be too condemning.

By the way, although it has been much faded by the years I still have my brother's Boro plastic rosette hanging on my wall, the Newcastle badge went out of the window years ago.

A deeply shame-faced Robert Shrug

Judgement: This is not only bad, it is BAD. If you are the type of lily-livered character who says he follows all the regions big three, you know to stick up for the northeast, then you'll have some sympathy for the man above. But I feel duty bound ladies and gentlemen of the jury to recommend only the harshest of punishments for this most appalling transgression. Hang him, hang him high.... What is that? There's no capital punishment anymore... but this is high treason, Treason against Teesside.

But hang on in there a minute, I've just realised that person is in fact none other than me, myself, I... err so I have perhaps been a tad hasty in my judgement. Can I just point out that I was not a fan of football and therefore Newcastle was the obvious choice... ha ha ha.... Not funny, eh?

Prepare the noose.

marooned on moon island

WE DUMP ALASTAIR BROWNLIE AND BERNIE SLAVEN ON THE DESERT ISLAND OF THE MOON

BERNIE

FIRST GAME
The first game for Boro was away at Leeds and Elland Road was an intimidating place to play after coming from Albion Rovers where the crowd numbered 200 and the odd haggis. My first home game was against Bradford and I still have the video of the match, and despite what Ali says I wasn't offside when I scored in front of the Holgate.

LAST GAME
I just keep the memory of my last home game which was against Manchester United and I managed to score past Schmeichel at the Holgate End. It was sad to end with a bitter taste but at least I can say that when I joined the team they were in Division Two and when I left they were in the Premiership.

PROUDEST MOMENT
It has to be the Rioch years when we went from liquidation to the top flight in successive seasons. I still remember winning promotion at Chelsea and after the game we were offered the chance to go to the Hilton for a meal but we decided to come home on the coach and had fish and chips with some fans by the motorway... it just summed up the bond between the fans and players.
I also remember getting to Wembley in the ZDS and Bruce praising my goal against Villa. It must have been some goal for Bruce to mention it...

ALASTAIR

FIRST TIME AT BORO
It was in the 1967 promotion season and I still remember the noise of the Holgate End and desperately wanting to be an Ayresome Angel. On the pitch the main player was John Hickton whose penalties were legendary taking his run up from Albert Park gates.

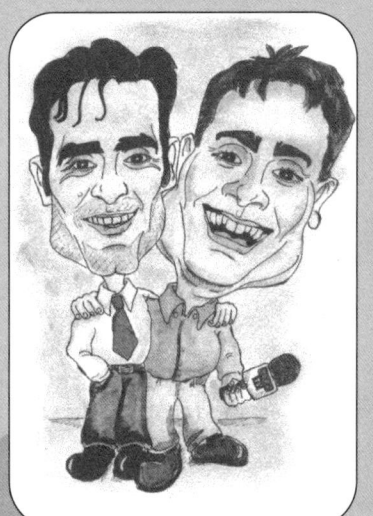

BEST TIME AS A FAN
As a young fan it was the cup run in 1970 getting to the FA Cup quarter final and John Hickton lobbing Alex Stepney to get us close to the semis. Sadly we lost the replay but it was a great cup run.
The play off win over Chelsea and the scenes in the Boro when the promotion parade brought the town to a standstill were superb and, naturally, commentating on the brilliance of Juninho.

WORST
No doubt liquidation. I spent hours listening to every radio news report on the final Friday just hoping that Boro would survive.

5 VIDEOS
1. The Bernie Slaven story to ensure that I would sleep well.
2. Juninho tribute to a legend to annoy Bernie if he came to visit.
3. 26 Septemeber 1970 Boro 6 QPR 2 Hickton and McIlmoyle at their destructive best.
4. Feb 14 1988 Boro 2 Villa 1 The Rioch revival years with Tony Mowbray's header summing up the team spirit.
5. April 13 1997 FA Cup semi final v Chesterfield. It was agony but brilliant cup football. One of the best ever cup matches.

MEMORABILIA
I still have my first Boro scarf with John Hickton badge.

PERSONALITY
It's got to be the living legend; I would worry about him too much if he were left alone to carry his own ego.

THEY PLAYED FOR MIDDLESBROUGH

Ken Barlow

Streetwise left winger Kenneth Barlow joined Middlesbrough straight from the University of life at the beginning of the swinging sixties and the way he swung in those left wing crosses was food and drink for twenty goal top scorer Ian Gibson. Unfortunately Barlow's brusque direct style was not to everyone's liking at the club, more than once he clashed with straight as a dye manager Raich Carter, while chairman **Albert Tatlock** was often heard to voice his misgivings over half a mild in the snug of his local.

Barlow forged the first of many partnerships, teaming up with ex Teddy Boy half-back Frank Spraggon for a formidable left flank. In one famous game in 1964 they had division 2 leaders Blackburn Rovers in a complete spin, running pint sized central defenders Newton and Ridley ragged. "It was enough to drive them to drink," wrote the Northern Echo's Ray Robertson. At the final whistle the Lancastrians and been soundly routed six nil, and for right back Stanley Ogden it was a personal nightmare, he'd never forget. Ogden had been turned inside out and more than once was left lounging on the seat of his pants. The Evening Gazette's Cliff Mitchell confided to his public that it was like "a street massacre," and "at times Barlow and Spraggon reduced Blackburn's play to pure soap opera." I'm sure everyone was in full agreement when he added, "we'll all look forward to the Rover's return match later in the season."

But the good times were not to last for Kenneth. Carter's successor Stan Anderson brokered a deal to exchange the young firebrand for a striker with a formidable reputation. It was left to Chairman Tatlock to introduce the new £50 000 signing in the most glowing terms, "Arthur Horsfield is better than Pele," he said in an address to the Ayresome Angels choral society.

For Barlow it was the start of a long and inglorious retreat through a myriad of failed partnerships with lower league clubs, leading eventually to an undignified midfield obscurity. It was while captain at lower league Oxford United that he branched out into a totally new direction. His chairman spotted potential in his captain's notes in the official programme and took him under his wing at his family newspaper business. After training Barlow would don his pac-a-mac and pick up his shorthand book, looking every inch the weathered leftfield reporter at the Daily Mirror.

Unfortunately Barlow was on the receiving end of the front pages himself when his ex-strike partner Dreary was imprisoned after being found guilty in a match-fixing ring. Barlow sprang into action sparking off a national campaign, utilising al his media contacts to the full to drive home the message, "Keep Dreary Behind Bars."

It was something of a shock reunion when Bryan Robson summoned the veteran Barlow back to Teesside at the start of this current campaign. For Barlow it was an emotional return to the Boro fold. Robson addressed the waiting reporters at a hastily convened press conference at Thornaby Station, "Kenny is a quality player and a local lad, and I am sure he will add real charisma to the side." Assistant manager Viv Anderson added, "we know all about Barl-ey, he is a super little player ....the boy's the last piece in the jigsaw... we now have the most experienced midfield in the league."

Ken Barlow is sponsored by Cadbury's cream eggs.

Rob Shrug

Players in the moon

PAUL KERR

FIRST GAME
v Preston in the FA Cup - not sure of the date. I had to go to Jack Hatfield's to get some of those astro boots. Might as well have worn ice skates. Ronnie Hindersley scored a 30 yarder. We got beat 1-0.

LAST GAME
Can't honestly remember. Was it against Millwall? Don't know - too painful.

WORST MOMENT
Getting bombed at Wembley. Picking splinters was bad enough but to then not get on... On about 80 minutes I looked at Toddy and said "Are you taking the piss or what?" He just ignored me.

BEST MOMENT
Easy. Promotion at Chelsea. We drank champagne in the dressing room then went into town and got thoroughly hammered. On the way home we stopped for fish & chips - washed down with champagne.

Another favourite moment was once when I was benched with Trevor Senior. Bruce looked across to Trevor and told him to warm up. Trevor just put his hands together and blew on them.

The FMTTM Millannual

81

BORO PLAYERS THROUGH THE AGES

Modern Middlesbrough fans might be vaguely aware of a couple of players being at the club before the signings of Gazza and Dean Gordon, but believe it or not that's just the tip of the iceberg - because, according to egg-headed boffins, the club has actually been in existance now for an incredible 123 years!!! Not to be outdone, FMTTM's top scholarly gentlemen Bob Fischer and Miniature G delved into the Boro's dusty anals and came over all historical with a sentimental look back at some of the clubs more, ahem, colourful servants...

1. VICTORIAN BOB SCRATCHITT (1890s)

A gentleman of the old school, invariably on match days Victorian Bob likes to breakfast with a fine shank of ham before promenading his way down to the old Paradise Ground via several flagons of ale in the Old Fanny Morgan and a selection of various legs of porks and tripe. Stopping only to relieve his sagging bladder against a gas lamp on the Linthorpe Road Monkey Parade, Victorian Bob hands handkerchieves to the ladies present to cover their eyes and noses, adjusts his Grimshaw and Sons Patented Pantaloon Fly Zip and pays his ha'penny to the gateman before pulling on his Brass-Bound Lace-Up Leather Toey-Knobbler Boots and participating in the noble art of Association Football. A fine practitioner of this ever-growing pastime, Bob's dazzling perambulations down the left-hand flank are halted only by the raising of his Domby and Son Gentleman's Top Hat at the beautiful ladies in the Archery Ground Parade Stand - that and the regular intervals in play for a fine display of marching by the Liverton Colliery Brass Band in the Paradise Ground centre-circle. And the final score - Middlesbrough Scabs 8, Burton Swifts 5 - is nothing less than a gentleman expects. Hurrah for Bob and Queen Vic herself. Hurrah! Hurrah! Hurrah!

2. LITTLE TOMMY ATKINS (1920s)

Unfortunately since plucky Tommy Atkins returned from active service in The Great War there seems to have been an important factor missing from his game... his left leg!!! Still, Tommy's been a revelation since manager Herbert Bamlett switched him to the right wing - and some of his crosses have left opposition players looking completely shellshocked. Mainly because that's exactly what they are. Still, with a wealth of International experience behind him (Tommy played in a hotly-contested "friendly" against the Bosch on Christmas Day) Tommy's future is burning brighter than the Hindenberg - he might have seen more than his fair share of mustard gas, but now he's cutting the mustard for "Borough" - and it's a REAL gas! And his supporters in the new-fangled slate-roofed Holgate End waste no time in giving him a sturdy round of applause - or at least they would if any of them had more than one hand left. In times of Great Depression for Boro, Tommy and his team-mates are used to "digging deep" and "entrenching" themselves across enemy lines - and with only six working legs in an eleven-man-squad that's quite "Somme" achievement - if that's not going too "Over the Top"!

3. FLASH HARRY WALKER (1950s)

Never let it be said that tricky Boro winger "Flash" Harry Walker (so called because of an alleged incident in Albert Park but it was never proved guv'nor, know what I mean, wink wink?) doesn't have a lot to offer. In fact from imported Cartier watches to the finest silky stockings, he's got the blimmin' lot! Pulling hard on a Strand Lonely Man and sidling his way to the Linthorpe Espresso Cafeteria, Flash Harry likes to prepare for the match with a frothy coffee and a jumping jive to Chas McFerris and his Sultans of Skiffle. And as for yellow cards - no way daddio! The only "book" Flash Harry's into is the one he's opened on today's result. He'll give you 6 to 4 on a 4-6 defeat, call it a monkey and Bob's your uncle, mister! Funny how the ball just seemed to slip through the keepers hands. Again. And again. And again. After the game Flash Harry likes to relax with a quiet drink with his friends - that's right, his friends Mr Morris the referee, Mr Halliwell and Mr Brown the linesmen and Councillor Duxbury from the Football Association. Mrs Halliwell after some sheer Pretty Pollys, Geoff? No problem for Flash Harry Walker. And how about a nice juicy steak for Lady Duxbury's pot, Sid? All friends together here. So never let it be said that football in the fifties isn't ahead of its time - in fact it's SO ahead of it's time that Flash Harry Walker can tell you next week's results... today! Get with it!

4. DIRTY DEREK BRACKEN (1970s)

Dirty Derek likes to pump himself up for the days match with a strut down to the ABC to watch "Confessions of a Ballcock Whoops! How's Your Father's Adventures, Mate?" before stopping off to neck a swift thirty seven pints of Twatney's Red Barrel at the Ferret and Cheesecloth on Southfield Road. Then it's straight on with the flared rubber suit and ready to give your all for Big Jack - and not only does that white-banded Boro shirt have Number Six on the BACK, it's got PLAYERS No.6 all down the front - Derek's barely got time to finish his first fag of the match when Boro are on the attack. Ninety minutes later, Boro are eighty-four points clear at the top of the second division, and it's time to party down in true seventies style. By six o'clock Dirty Derek is letting his hair down in no uncertain terms and when Derek's hair gets let down it hits the ground with a thump - trimming sidechoppers the size of a subcontinent and dowsing his manly flab with Brute 501, Derek polishes off a couple of bottles of Blue Nun from Winterschladen, then it's off to the Club Marimba, boogie to Baccara, and the keys to his spanking P-reg Capri are on the bar just waiting to be picked up by a nubile Kathy Secker. This is where the big nobs hang out, alright - just ask Alan Willey about that!

The FMTTM Millannual

5. BIG GIANFRANCO RISOTTO (1990s)

Italian superstar Gianfranco is living proof that money can't buy you happiness - he might be earning £175,000 a millisecond at the new, Riverside Revolution Boro, but that's scant consolation for off-the-field problems that have become so intense that, after two seasons, he still hasn't played a match for his beloved new side. Speaking out in top Italian newspaper Gazetta Moronica, the man fans of his former club ACDC Milan nicknamed "Il Casco Viola" ("The Purple Helmet") explained, "My mind it is a swilling cesspool in the beating heart of unconsciousness. At Middlesbrough I find my true self, my one self, the beauty in which my heart has opened, but on the other hand I wouldn't mind playing for Tottingham Hotspurs. Anyroadup I must stay in Italia while my canary, Fritz, receives treatment from Dr Hofmeister of Berlin for chronic haemerrhoids. I send the Middlesbrough fans my love, and Bob Ward he is my amigo" A meticulously strict teetotaller, Gianfranco prepares himself for Boro matches by walking in the hills around his childhood village of Colonica, thinking about his mother and speaking on a mobile phone to his agent Paulo Tagliatelle, who also happens to be his cousin, his brother-in-law, his doctor and, by a bizarre coincidence, chief scout for Atletico Madrid. A club for whom Gianfranco has recently expressed his "deep respect and admiration. Not like those tossers in Middlesbrough. Ooops - sorry, boys, can we leave that bit out? No? Oh dear." Gianfranco has, however, recently pledged his future to the Boro in an exclusive interview with Eric Paylor in the Evening Gazette.

---

marooned on moon island
ANTHONY VICKERS
Evening Gazette

FIVE MATCH VIDEOS

1 Boro 2 Port Vale 2 (Div 3, Aug 86) - back from the brink Boro begin a football fairytale at Pool's Victoria Ground.
Plenty of time to scour the tape slo-mo frame by frame matching the faces of the 3,690 diehards in the crowd to the 33,000 who now claim to have been there.

2 Boro 2 Man City 1 (Rumbelows Cup, Dec 91) - that eerie night match in the fog in which grey shadowy figures loomed out the mist momentarily then faded away again. It would be nice to finally know what actually happened beyond the edge of the Holgate End penalty box.

3 Coventry 3 Boro 4 (Div 1, Oct 88) - Bernie's finest hour: also the chance to watch him fight it out with fiery fellow hat-trick man David Speedie over the match-ball.

4 Boro 3 Chesterfield 3 (FA Cup semi, Old Trafford Apr 97) - possible the most dramatic match ever: plucky ten man minnows come from behind to dramatically clinch a replay thanks to a Geoff Hurst style goal being ruled out by comedy ref. Highly entertaining.

5 Boro 6 Derby 1 (Prem, Mar 97) - the height of Boro's Foreign Legion Golden Age: Rav, Emo and the Little Feller at their very best, teasing the faithful into thinking it was still possible to escape the drop. Not quite, but some fantastic football.

MEMORABILIA

a) the old Dial-a-Duck Ayresome away dug-out would make a neat shelter and double as a goal for kickabouts on the beach.

b) the old "Brucie Requests..." sign, a constant source of amusement, would make a good target for missile throwing practice and the material for a raft when I got bored in paradise.

BORO PERSON

I considered ace angler Big Jack to keep me in fish suppers or axe hero Robbie Mustoe to throw some guitar shapes around the beach campfire, but in the end it had to be Gazza.

Lets face it, no matter how lost and isolated this island is, with the maverick media magnet around sooner or later the lads from The Sun are bound to find you.

FAN-TASY FOOTBALL

This modern game of Association Football is a strange beast. Once the private property of the working class masses, it has grown beyond all control to transcend the class system and become the favourite pastime of kings, queens, dodgy politicians and fading celebrities. The massive influx of tv cash has transformed football from a humble game into a mega entertainment industry. And yet it remains 'the people's game.' But for which people? Where do you fit into the grand scheme of things? Are you a 'pro-Super Leaguer,' an 'anti-World Clubber' or a 'sit-on-the-fence Jimmy Hiller?' Do you long for Lineker or dote on Des? Do you favour Ferguson or revere Robson? Well, take our little test and discover where you stand. Or sit, post Taylor.

1. How do you spend your spare time?
A. Sticking my Panini sitckers in the album. And rearranging my David Beckham posters. And buying replica shirts.
B. Watching the lads home and away. Or watching the reserves and the juniors in the hope that one day I'll get to run the line.
C. Pulling the wings off flies.

2. You see an old lady struggling to cross a busy road. What do you do?
A. Run across the road in case she beats me to the pointless accessories shop and buys the last remaining Ryan Giggs pencil sharpener.
B. Help her across. You never know, she might be a long time fan and have seen all the greats play and have loads of stories about the Boro all those years ago.
C. Push her into the traffic.

3. What's your favourite colour?
A. Red. And white. With black socks.
B. Red. Boro Red.
C. Black.

4. Your mother is in hospital. You go to visit her. What do you take with you for her to read?
A. My brand new Andy Cole 'Guide to Better Finishing' book with a lock of Peter Schmeichel's hair on the inside cover.
B. The Juninho book, the Jackie Charlton book, Cloughie's autobiography, and my Boro scrapbooks 1973-1999.
C. The Co-op Funerals Guide.

5. You are given £50 for your birthday. How do you spend it?
A. Buy the compete Champions League Supporter kit, including scarf, rattle, flick-knife, and posters of all the star players.
B. Buy the home shirt, away shirt, shorts, socks and bobble hat for the bairn's Action Man.
C. Buy drink.

6. How will you spend your summer holiday?
A. Playing football with my friends. I'll be Dwight Yorke and beat everyone with my super finishing.
B. A weekend away after the season, then get sorted for pre-season friendlies.
C. Poisoning the local cats.

7. Where did you watch August's solar eclipse?
A. In my garden. I wore my 'Jaap Stam Eclipse Buster' sunglasses so my eyes were perfectly protected because nothing gets past Jaappy.
B. On the spot where I used to stand in the Holgate, cos it was such a momentous moment. Until the wifey chased me off her patio.
C. With my myopia, every day's an eclipse.

A's Ah yes, the modern fan. Man Utd 'til you die - or if they stop winning things. You will own all the merchandise, be able to name every player from the last 2 seasons, haven't missed a match since March 1998 (apart from the ones not televised of course) and you go to sleep dreaming of Man Utd glory years - 1997-1999 (apart from Arsenal winning the title in the middle there - but that doesn't really count). You are a bandwagon jumping, media controlled, pseudo fan. Man Utd deserve you.

B's You are what supporters were like when Grandad were a lad. Cut you and you bleed red and white, etc, etc. You know Boro will always leave you wanting, but your father went, and his father before him, and his mother before him, and so there's no way you're getting out of it. You cherish The Power Game theme, worship at an onyx Alan Foggon (that's a lot of onyx), and haven't missed a match since you were two.

C's You are perfect. We need you. Please get in touch:

Philip Don, Referees Association c/o F.A., Lancaster Gate, London W1

marooned on moon island
SIMON O'ROURKE - TYNE TEES

- MY TOP FIVE BORO MATCHES.

1. v Sunderland (A) 16th Jan 1994
Boro lost two - one. Memorable for me because I had a ticket but couldn't go as my dad broke his leg on the morning of the match.

2. v Burnley (H) 13th August 1994
Boro won two - nil. Robbo's first match in charge - you could smell the green shoots of recovery.

3. v Aston Villa (H) 3rd May 1997
Summed up the most ridiculous season in football history. Two - nil up. Threw that away. Then Ravanelli penalty won it in injury time. Kept the pot boiling until Elland Road.

4. v Liverpool (H) 18th Feb 1998
Coca Cola Semi-Final 2nd leg. Boro back to Wembley. Branca (Gawd bless 'im) arrived in style. Just a class occasion and a class match.

5. v Oxford (H) 3rd May 1998
Promotion - always good for a laugh. Spoke to Nigel Pearson afterwards. He's normally this big rock hard scary bloke - but he was well choked up.

MY TOP BORO ITEM.......... tough one.
Probably the Satay sticks at the half time buffet against Portsmouth at the Riverside in 1997.

DESERT ISLAND BORO BLOKE.
This is a really dodgy question by the way. Probably Ravanelli - so I could spend eternity telling him what a Tw*t he is.

G-R-E-A-T BORO MOMENTS

FRANK SPRAGGON

SPRAGGON'S REVENGE ON THE CHICKEN RUN BOO BOYS!

Frank Spraggon was a stalwart of Boro's tight-fisted defence of Charton's Champions - Peter Brine recently described Frank as a "great defender" and and that before moving into his familiar left back berth he had been an "unbelievable sweeper." Few would argue with Frank's defensive pedigree apart from, of course, the several hundred self-appointed boo-boys in the old South Terrace "Chicken Run" who would mercilessly barrack Frank whenever he played on their side.

Now, and for one night only, Frank Spraggon finally gets even with the long-bulldozed Chicken Run. Squawk!

The FMTTM Millannual

runes of the game

by Mark Drury

"Mark" they said, "tell us your vision of the Boro in 100 years time." There's a nice easy one. I mean, I don't know what I'm having for dinner tomorrow so how the hell should I know what the Boro are going to be doing in a century? Bloody editors…

Anyway, for what it's worth, here are my considered opinions on the next 100 years of Middlesbrough FC (i.e., I'll type the first thing that comes into my head).

1) It's a pretty safe bet that Bryan Robson should still be in charge. Governments have been telling us for the last 20 years that there's no such thing as a job for life but don't you believe it! Our Bryan's as safe as houses. Big futuristic houses that is.

2) Alan Moore will still be considered a "good prospect" in 2099. "He just needs to find a bit of consistency." One for the future indeed.

3) Eric Paylor will still be awarding the stars in the Gazette as follows: *** Andy Townsend, ** Robbie Mustoe, * Steve Vickers (for trying, bless him).

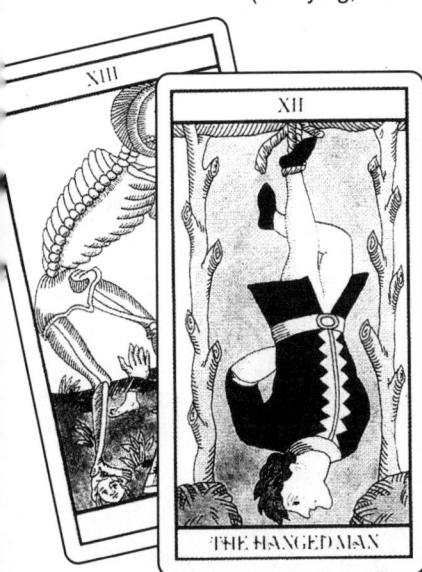

4) 2099 will be the year we return to Ayresome Park at the behest of the new Club owners, the Dicken family. The reason given will be that it is an attempt to return to the Club's roots and recapture the lost atmosphere of times gone by. The real reason will be that Newboulds want the pie-selling franchise back. And it gives them the perfect excuse to bulldoze the house of a certain fanzine editor. All in favour raise their right hands… motion passed.

5) In an effort to improve our faltering youth set-up, Boro become the first team to sign a foetus. Scouts spotted the young sprog's talent after seeing the pregnant mother doubled up in pain as the little blighter practised his goal kicks in the amniotic sac. Well, you have to catch 'em young or they'll all get signed by Villa.

6) 2099 sees the glorious return of the tradition of half time penalty competitions. 100 years of dancing girls and crap singers proved too much to take. By the way, anybody remember that competition where you had to kick a football through the window of a cardboard cut-out car? Well whatever happened to the car, because I don't remember anyone winning it? Was there ever a car to be won? Anyone care? Oh, I'll get on with it then. Anyway, as tradition dictates, the penalties will still be appallingly executed but incredibly entertaining nevertheless. And the fat kid will always bury his penalty before baring his huge gut at the away fans. The finest example of this was the fat lad who took a penalty for St David's at half time in the Premier League game against Blackburn back in 1992-93. Were you that Jabba? Have you thinned down yet? Why do I remember it all so vividly? Probably all that bare flesh. My knees are trembling at the very memory.

7) Under new Premier League rules, it will be compulsory for every club to sign at least one boy band member. As Man Utd seem to have a team full of them at present they will have the advantage. This is a move designed to appeal to the pre-pubescent girl market. Robbie Stockdale being an early forerunner of the concept. Looks like a reject from Boyzone doesn't he? And we all know what they say about members of Boyzone don't we? They can't sing for toffee? Oh, you thought I meant something else....

8) Eric Paylor will still be telling the fans that the "last piece in the jigsaw" is about to be signed and it'll probably be Carlton Palmer's slightly less talented grandson. If we're lucky.

9) Alastair Brownlee will be forced to accept that at the age of 126, there is absolutely no chance of a return to the "Super Cellnet Riverside Stadium" for Juninho. (One you got wrong Mark! Ed)

10) Alastair Brownlee will be strung up for saying the "The Super Cellnet Riverside Stadium" for the thousandth time in one sentence.

11) We will still have won sod all.

12) Against all the odds Boro have become THE team to support. Glamorous, dashing, exciting, they will win the hearts and minds of the whole country with their own special brand of free-flowing, attacking football, the like of which has never been seen in Europe before. And they'll get relegated. Probably.

Well, you can't expect things to change all that much over the course of a century. This is my vision of the future and there is nothing you can do to change it, for I am the Oracle. I see all, and nought escapes my all-embracing gaze. Tremble at the future, for it is exactly the same as the past! I have spoken. Oh and I nearly forgot this one. Bob Fischer's Donkeywatch column will be exactly the same as the previous fortnight's, and the fortnight before that and the one before that. In fact, the same as it has been for a century or more. And still they read him! The fools!
Finally, theologians will determine that Purgatory is a Boro season ticket that renews itself every year. Nowt like a bit of optimism is there?

Marooned on moon island

JIM KNIGHT (BBC)

FIVE MATCH VIDEOS
1. Man Utd v Boro. Premier League 1998 Old Trafford 2-3 to Boro
2. Boro v Newcastle Coca Cola 1996 Riverside 3-1 to Boro
3. Boro v Chesterfield FA Cup 1997 Old Trafford 3-3 draw.
4. Boro v Chelsea 1st leg of Play Off final at Ayresome 1988 Boro win 2-0 (ultimately win 2-1 to go up at home to cockney, pitch-invading, scumbags).
5. Boro v Leeds 2nd Division Ayresome 1988 2-0 to Boro (Pally scored with an overhead kick!).

MEMORABILIA
My cracked, ageing, leather flying jacket - splashed, stained and slashed with all the memories of hundreds of Boro adventures across the land. OR - a linesman's flag to remind me of Bernie.

BORO PERSON
It'd have to be Merse. Firstly cos I've always fancied myself as a bit of an amateur psychologist, and who better, in isolation, to practise my skills on? Secondly, he'd be sure to have some mind-bending drugs with him to help us break the boredom. And thirdly, on a quaff-free desert island, who better to help me cope with my endless quest for more beer?

FIRST MATCH
Sat on grandad's knee, in the North Stand at Ayresome, at the tender age of seven (approx 1967). Can remember very little, but have strong memories of the acrid smell of cigarettes and oxo and of how green the pitch was! Eric McMordie and Gordon Jones feature in the memory too, but I couldn't even be sure if they were playing!

BEST MEMORY
A) Me and Tim are sat at Old Trafford, surrounded by thousands of the richest, spoiltest, fans in the world. We're already doubting our sanity cos Boro are two nought up. Suddenly, it's Deano to Ricard, Ricard back to Deane, first time shot, Schmeichel on his arse, ball bulges the onion bag. I look at Tim - he looks at me - it can't be! We stand as one - and re-enact the last dance of the mohicans - tears in our eyes. It's Man United nil Boro three - wake up soft lad!

B) We're at Wembley - can you believe it? We're Boro fans and we're at Wembley - in a proper cup final. It's been a tense, over-cautious game, but suddenly the little Brazilian fella's got a chance to run at Leicester. He jinks and weaves.. we're all standing now..begging for him to make it happen........ but he loses it.....and it spins out to Rav.
Whack!
It went in, and back out, so fast we simply couldn't believe it. Did it? Didn't it?... YES..he's got his fr***in shirt over his head..we're goin' mad. The singing and the dancing just got louder and louder.. "SUPA supa Rav, SUPA, supa Rav etc etc..." There were just a couple of minutes left as I turned to Reevey and yelled - "not even the fr****n Boro can spoil this for me now................"

WORST MEMORY
10 seconds after the above - that Heskey kid!

The FMTTM Millannual

and in a packed programme tonight...
Bob Fischer cuts snippets of genius from the Boro's match programmes of yesteryear

1980: DAVID ARMSTRONG'S TESTIMONIAL "SHOWBIZ" XI

Showbiz XI

From:

Cecil Humphries
(TV personality. His recent series was The Buccaneer)
Rolando Ugolini
(Special guest. Ex-Middlesbrough goalkeeper)
Bryan Marshall
(Captain Tony Blair of the Bucaneer)
Brendan Price
(Det. Sgt. Bonney of Target)
Bill Oddie
(The little hairy one in the Goodies)
Billy Boyle
(Mr. Billy of Basil "Boom Boom" Brush)
Roy North
(Mr. Roy from the Basil Brush show and Get It Together)
Tony Rance
(Ex-professional footballer, now West Brom general manager)
Doug Fielding
(Sgt. Quilley of Z cars)
Billy Hartman
(GBH from TV's Oh Boy)
Ken Farrington
(Billy Walker of Coronation Street)
Miki Anthony
(Records for RCA with many successful records to his name)
John Lyons
(From Spooner's Patch, On The Busses and Z Cars)
Kevin O'Shea
(Founder member of the team, ex-Limerick City)
Nobby Brackett
(Trainer and sponge man, from Z cars)
Tony Trent
(TV and film personality. Latest film McVicar)
Johnny Cohen
(Commentator — and entertainer)

V

New Durham (First half)
Durham Boilers (Second half)

(Both teams are coached by David Armstrong)

Showbiz Star Bill Oddie

Referee for Showbiz match is Neil Midgley, a personal friend of David Armstrong

Kick-off 6.30 p.m.
Referee: **Neil Midgley** (Manchester)
Linesmen:
Tom Radigan (Hartburn)
Mike Birt (Redcar)

Disturbingly reminiscant of the "Showbiz" XI that visits Slade Prison in Porridge: The Movie - "a weatherman, nine small parts and a Widow Twankey." Young girls all over Teesside must have trembled in their nylon knickers at the thought of Miki Anthony treading their hallowed turf - "Many succesful records to his name"? I guess they must be thinking of "If It Wasn't For the Reason That I Love You" which reached No. 27 in February 1973. Add to that John Lyons from the legendary Spooner's Patch, Captain Tony Blair (!) and Cecil Humphries from The Buccaneer, Rolando Ugolini and "The little hairy one in The Goodies" and you can only presume that Hollywood had to close down for the week beginning the 1st of October 1980 with so much of its prime talent away at Spike's testimonial. Can I have your autograph please, erm, sorry who are you again?

RAV'S RANT
This millennium . . . . Football in the next millennium

I have been thinking, something you Eenglish know nothing about, ha ha ha. What will happen in the next millennium in the game of football. Well, obviously, the glorious Italia will continue to dominate the world game. You Eenglish will no doubt fail to qualify for most of the championships - you may get to another quarter-final or something but that will only be because of some referee or linesman who has, how you say, lost the pot. And you will still be whinging and being miserable like you Eenglish always are. And another thing. The Champions' League will expand so that there will be more opportunity for the Italian teams to thrash you Eenglish, even if you might have eight teams in the league. But one thing is for sure - Middlesburg will not be in it. And they will not win the FA Cup or anything else. Now if I was still there and they got rid of all those Eenglish players, there might be a chance. What Middlesburg needs is more Italian players. But anyway, how you say, I digest. What was I saying? Ah, yes. Football in the new millennium. My final prediction comes from Stampy who told me this before I left. He said, I think, that the Mackems were a shower of Sprite who have as much chance of winning anything as the Geordies have of having a realistic opinion of the size of their club. I will take Stampy's word for it because that was the longest sentence he ever put together while I was at Middlesburg. You Eenglsih, I don't know . . . .

The FMTTM Millannual

90

Riverside Rocky High

Cory Muzyka describes how a native Canadian came to fall head over heels for the Boro. This is the story of his first actual date with the Riverside, last season.

It was a cold winter afternoon when we drove over the Pennines to Middlesbrough. The three hours from Preston had seemed like an eternity, but compared to home this was nothing. In Canada you could drive for hours and see nothing but endless mountains and prairie. As I directed my fiancé from the AA road map and saw the distances on the road signs becoming smaller, I realised that I was edging closer and closer to a dream I'd held so dear in my heart for such a long time. People have often asked me what it was that drew me to support Boro. How can it be that a lad from Vancouver on Canada's West Coast could be interested in a football club from an industrial town in the North East of England? Supporting your club in England is something a person is either born to, in the same way that a child receives a family name, or something you acquire over a period of time. I sensed a pride in a town whose football club was not just in their veins or their pockets but in their hearts. A team that doesn't always win but a team that has a soul and waits with anticipation for its first big win.

As I looked across the open moorland I thought of my old friend back home who had first introduced me to Middlesbrough. He was born in Vancouver, strangely enough, the son of an English couple that had immigrated here from the North East years ago. His parents must have done a good job because I've never met anyone quite so proud of their country or their heritage. His passion for a town and country he's really never lived in seemed alive and this rubbed off on me, the Canadian boy. I remembered a stuffed bear he had in his apartment, it was all dressed up in an old Boro kit. I used to listen to him romancing for hours about England and this had become a part of me too. I laughed to myself now, just before we left, I had met Ian for a drink and he'd said to me "Cory, Teesside really is the pits, full of chemical works, you know!" The funny thing was that I didn't care, I wanted to go to this place that a friend of mine called 'home' and felt so strongly about. I wanted to capture some of the spirit, I guess.

Going to watch the football in Canada is an interesting experience, which I have to tell people about, as it really is quite a performance. First of all we have to wait for the Boro's turn to come around which is once in a blue moon on Sportsnet if we're lucky. As folks are quite aware the earth rotates, as a result us poor buggers over here on the Pacific coast are 8 hours behind the regular time in Britain. If a game kicks off at 3pm we have to drag our lazy arses out of bed at around 6am. Sneak out of the house without waking anyone up and find somewhere like the British Ex Serviceman's Club to watch the game. Bleary eyed, we have to sit there for a full 90 minutes and be content with the enjoyment of the game because no one can get a beer at that time of day. If for some reason Sky decide that they are going to move the time of the game to suit the lucky people with Sky Sports over in England, we can be getting up to watch the game as early as 4am! My first live game was like that, I remember us drawing that game with Chesterfield at 5am. We were all sitting in front of the TV shouting encouragement across the ocean when the entire city was still sleeping. My mate and I drove home, in stunned silence, as the city awoke. It was quite a strange experience, and one I'll never forget.

By now, we were nearing the Travel Lodge at Sedgefield, which was where we were booked in for our three night stay. It seemed a long way out of town but it was good for what we wanted although I wouldn't recommend the Little Chef. That laughing little bastard took all of my money! After getting settled in there we made our way into town, it was dark by then as I tried desperately to pick the way from the map to "The Star and Garter" which was where we were meeting some of the people from the mailing list. We seemed to have passed a lot of chemical works all lit up in the darkness and I was trying to find the Transporter Bridge, which Ian had told me, was a famous landmark in the town. After passing one sign we could see it on the horizon, all blue steel and not even working. We found the pub without too much difficulty and met up with everyone. It was so nice to eventually put faces to the names of people who'd become my transatlantic friends - Albat, Sal, Mike, Dave, Rob... all totally brilliant!

The following day I was awake bright and early, today was the day I had been waiting for ever since I'd ran to our mailbox and the letter from Diane O'Connell at the ticket office had landed in my hand. Now I was looking at the letter and thinking about the tickets for the afternoon game with West Ham. For the first time ever I wouldn't be seeing the sunrise on the way to the game, I would be actually be going there with all the fans and soaking up the atmosphere. After wrapping myself up warm in what seemed like a dozen sweaters - bright red Boro home kit on the top of course - we made our way to the Riverside. I wanted to get there early to pick up the tickets and wait for the players to arrive. When I saw the ground, like an oasis in the wasteland, I realised what I had been waiting for all these years and almost had to pinch myself because I was actually there. This wasn't TV!

My fiancé and I were a bit nervous about the car her mother had leant us for the trip and we both laughed when we pulled into the parking lot and a big burly bloke said, "you watch the match and we'll watch your car." I think "you watch the match and we'll nick your car" would have been a better choice of words. The gamble did pay off and she was pleasantly surprised to see that it was still there, and intact, afterwards. It was such a feeling of euphoria as we marched our way through the crowds of people, through security and straight up the front desk at the ground. Diane came down and handed us our tickets, programmes, key rings and scarves, which we thought was extremely generous of them especially as we were only expecting the tickets. We went back outside and I ran around getting as many autographs as possible whilst Kate took pictures of me with people like Hamilton Ricard, Robbie Mustoe and Dean Gordon. We went inside and got ourselves nicely settled in to our seats in the upper tier of the West Stand. I had rather fancied myself in the North Stand, but I know we got a good view from where we were. I had learnt most of the songs, and took great pride in being able to shout (amongst other things) "come on Boro" and "we love you Boro..." with the rest of the people in the ground.

I think one of the disappointing things about the match was about 10 minutes into the game when whole loads of West Ham fans were seated with us. Apparently, they should have been in the Cellnet suite and weren't properly dressed so they had been stuck outside with us. I was trying to watch Robbie Stockdale take a corner, and couldn't see because they were all stood up. I got brave (mainly because all around me were Boro, except this lot) and asked if they could please sit down. They shouted back at me "You'll never score from there, mate!" I'm not one to deny anyone a beer but these chaps shouldn't have been there because they had been drinking all the way from Cellnet headquarters in Reading. They were all plastered and took great joy in insulting as many Boro fans and players as possible. After all the things Kate had told me about violence at football games, you would have hoped that security would have moved them but they didn't.

Still it didn't marr my joy as 10 minutes later, from a Dean Gordon corner on the other side, Brian Deane rose above the defenders and headed past Shaka Hislop. I jumped to my feet and shouted "Get in there you beauty!" taking notice of the disheartened Hammers in front.

A great moment occurred when Hamilton Ricard was substituted... I stood up and started clapping as I thought he had a good game (and questioning why Robbo was taking him off), and in unison so did everyone else! I starting shouting "Ricard! Ricard!" and he waved happily to the supporters as we all sang his name. I really felt like I was at home.

One of the funniest things that happened was when we were standing outside after the match, talking to some mates, and the door flew open and Gazza ran right past me through the car park. One little lad shouted after him "That's the fastest we've seen you run all day Gazza!" It was great to get into the car and hear all the post match commentary on the radio as we drove away from the ground.

Sunday was my birthday and I was pleased to be spending it nowhere else but in the North East. Kate and I went down to Whitby and then to see a couple of my friends, one of them was a lady called Anne who rather kindly has sent me Boro shirts in the past and another was in Newcastle. It was nice to know that I had friends all those thousands of miles away from home that welcomed me in as if I'd known them forever. Finally, we had to leave on the Monday but not before we had been back to the Riverside for a tour of the ground. It was like a pilgrimage for me, sitting in Gibbo's chair, standing on the pitch side and looking around the changing rooms. There was even a note still pinned to the door about Gazza's set up with the News of the World streakers the week before.

Our last port of call was Rockcliffe Park, we arrived too late to see any training but it had a peace and tranquillity about it that I loved. The old house alongside this brand new training complex. I stood in the drizzle and looked out across the fields and felt happy that my dream had come true but also sad because we were leaving. If it wasn't for Middlesbrough FC (internet) mailing list I wouldn't have met my wife, and one day I will take my son or daughter back there and show them a real football game not soccer as they call it here...

Cory Muzyka

---

marooned on moon island
BERNARD GENT

FIVE VIDEOS / COMMENTARIES
Riverside Revolution -- Juninho -- The TFM commentary of the Data Systems Final by courtesy of Gent, Mills and Brian Laws, the FIRST time Boro were at Wembley -- **The Helmet Rides Again** (Chubby Brown). He is red and white, through and through -- **Gazza's goofs and gaffs, Referee.**

MEMORABILIA
As you would expect, Radio Ayresome re-invented! That would mean having the broadcast 'box' complete with the lid which was handy if the fans were unhappy with the team and started throwing things!! Also: The Ayresome mike, the Ayresome bovril, wembley ticket stub and most of all, the Power Game casette/record.

BORO PERSON
Player - Graeme Souness; Manager - John Neal / Bryan Robson.

FIRST MATCH
December 7, 1946, Boro 2 Arsenal 0

BEST MEMORY
1 Boro's goalkeeper, Dave Cumming sent off for punching the Arsenal player, Leslie Compton. It was as good a punch as any top-class boxer -knocked him out cold. Went up to punch the ball...
and bingo!! I can remember it as if it was yesterday.

2 Watching Wilf Mannion and comparing this with the wonderment of Juninho.

WORST MEMORY
Getting within a minute of winning the cup at Wembley but going to a replay which we lost to Leicester (our bogey team) when, if we had used the substitute system properly, we could have slowed down the pace of the game and even wasted enough time to have won it.

No Action Replay

Boro exile from birth - Geoff Vickers looks back over his years with the Boro and tells the Riverside rookies all about the legacy of Dickie Rooks, Jimmy Hill the summer of '73 and a time when Boro were never on the box.

I am not sure many thirtysomethings can remember in much detail the first game they saw Boro play back in the 1960's. Perusal of the numerous Boro history books which have hit the market over the past few years will no doubt jog a few memories of that first fateful meeting of the Club and soon to be committed fan.

I am not sure why I should remember seeing Boro play for the very first time beyond the fact that it was not at Ayresome Park but at Bloomfield Road, Blackpool one Saturday afternoon deep in the heat of the 1968-69 season. Boro earned a 1-1 draw thanks to an equaliser from the bald head of Dickie Rooks, a granite built George Heslop look-a-like centre half. It wasn't so much the match, which was memorable, indeed it was the sort of game which made even my dad ask for the final whistle - five minutes into the first half! No, what made this match stick in the brain was the fact that it was broadcast nationally on Match of The Day later that evening.

Younger fans probably won't appreciate how exciting the prospect of Boro on TV really was back in those days. No Sky, no live games, no "Boro TV" on Comcast cable television, no foreign stars, no interest really beyond the Boro diehards who found the prospect of Boro being on Match of The Day in those pre satellite days as enthralling as, well, Christmas day morning or Fireworks night.

I grew up in Manchester and Cheshire and mention of Middlesbrough in the local media was about as rare as a strand of hair on Dickie Rook's pate. I used to watch Football Preview avidly as a child. The forerunner to Football Focus on Grandstand on Saturday afternoons was fronted by a fat Scotsman called Sam Leitch. A pronounced Scottish tongue, Leitch very rarely got his vocal chords around the pronunciation of Middlesbrough so when he did one Saturday afternoon my eyes lit up. It was that strange little moment which made me realise that I was a Boro fanatic! Boro you see were very rarely televised and when the days of video came out in the 1980's I took full advantage. When in the third division in 1987 I bought the full-length video of Boro's 4-1 win at Rotherham at Millmoor. I still have it today although it must now rank about as interesting as a three-hour fishing video. Not to me!!

Dickie Rooks - Taught Bobby Charlton everything he knew about comb-overs

The bizarre choice for MOTD of Blackpool versus Middlesbrough in the old first division was puzzling. Neither side was challenging at the top of the league - but it was important to me because it was the first time a Tyne Teesless supporter could watch his beloved team on the screen.

Boro were never to really feature again on BBC as a main match until Jack Charlton had taken the reigns over from Stan Anderson back in the Summer of 1973. By Christmas of that year Boro were already being crowned Champions elect, so good were they. Aston Villa at Villa Park were to be one of the sterner tests that season and sure enough BBC MOTD cameras decided to go for the first and only time to a Boro game that season. Again it was to be an unmemorable 1-1 draw. John Craggs scored direct from a freekick, which was deflected. But Jimmy Hill decided to dwell not on Boro's powerful midfield of Souness, Murdoch and Armstrong, but had a carp at Jack Charlton's

93

somewhat shocking tactic (when one looks back on it now) of Boro killing time by holding the ball up at the opposition's corner flag. Hickton and Foggon, presumably because of their physique, were normally employed to take a short corner, turn their back on play and hold the ball in the corner segment. Invariably too this would wind up the opposition to the point of an inevitable scuffle. It certainly wound up Jimmy Hill who said that football had no place for such cynicism. But, then again, when did Whor Jackie's tactics seek to court media favour?

BBC lack of interest certainly wound up us Boro fans in the seventies. Why should MOTD constantly overlook a team regularly in the top ten in the top division? It accounted for the occasional chant of Jimmy Hill's a b**stard and something even stronger when the cameras did come to show their customary ten mins of highlights. On Boro's return to the top flight in 1974, MOTD came to Ayresome Park twice that season in the league. Boro did not score in either game against Newcastle United (0-0) or Leeds United (0-1). The latter defeat was as a result of Alan Clarke's goal of the season. It is a goal which is punctuated with the Holgates chant of "Your Going To Get your f...." well you know the rest. You can still relive that moment on BBC Match of The Day Boro video - uncensored!!! But the magic that is television was to come in the form of Middlesbrough v Sunderland FA Cup 4th Round in January 1975. I was swaying in the middle of the chicken run that day. Infact if one was to ask me to list the top five most Boro exciting games that I was at that list would be as follows

1) Boro v Chesterfield - FA CUP Semi Final 1997
2) Boro v Derby County - FA Cup Quarter Final 1997
3) Boro v Swansea - FA Cup 3rd Round 1981
4) Boro v Newcastle - Division 2 1991
5) Boro v Sunderland - FA Cup 4th Round 1975

You will notice that four of those five games were FA CUP matches - easily the best competition in the world and one which has no competition when it comes to thrills and memories.

Anyway back to the Sunderland Cup Tie and a game played in the strongest gale imaginable. Boro scored three goals in front of MOTD cameras that day - forget the fact that two were penalties but even then the BBC sent their third string commentator to cover the match; one Alan Weeks, the 1970's version of Ray Stubbs and better known as a Swimming commentator.

Over the next few seasons MOTD did show a number of Boro games. All of them unremarkable and inevitably the third game on anyway. There was one exception to that in 1980 when Norwich City visited Boro and were promptly thumped 6-1 and in front of BBC cameras!! After that the magic that was Boro on Match of The Day went.

Since those heady days that were my introduction to supporting Boro, Bob Wilson has come and gone on Football Focus, Alan Weeks has sadly passed away, every Boro goal is televised and a clip is shown on MOTD, and I can read all that I want to know about the Boro from my home in Hertfordshire on the Internet. But it is back thirty years that I cast my mind to. When TV was a world of fantasy, not a business, and when you could always say Boro would never be on MOTD you didn't really mind because you never knew any different. I sometimes hear supporters complain about media coverage on Boro and I smile. Yes it may reflect the fact that Southern bias views Boro as unfashionable - even today. But it is a hell of a lot better than when I was a boy.

Geoff Vickers

G-R-E-A-T BORO MOMENTS

GARY GILL "RUNS IT OFF"

On the 8th of April 1989, two minutes into a crucial relegation clash at home to Southampton, Boro midfielder Gary "Gonzo" Gill crashed with a sickening crunch into veteran Saints custodian John "Budgie" Burridge. Grown men right across the Holgate winced into their Bovril, but one man surprisingly unconcerned was long-serving Boro physio Tommy Johnson. "Go on son, you'll soon run it off" advised Dr Doolittle to our hero after a quick once-over with the magic sponge. Unfortunately ten more minutes of limping after the ball soon convinced Gilly that this was ONE injury that would take more than a dab of cold water and a pat on the shoulder to cure. Not surprising, really - he had a badly broken leg and hardly ever played for us again. Ouch!

The FMTTM Millannual

mss
Middlesbrough Supporters South

In 1975 a handful of **exiled Boro fans** gathered on the steps to the entrance of Arsenal's main stand to form what is now **Middlesbrough Supporters South.** Twenty five years on, there are over 800 members spread around Britain and the world, from brickies to bank managers, teachers to MPs, clerks to managing directors, police officers to on-the-run-from-MI5 intelligence officers, all with one indelible link, **a love for Middlesbrough Football Club.** Many were born on Teesside and still have the accent (or traces of it!) and some are second or even third generation Boro fans, born in London *with* (whisper it) Cockney accents. Over seventy are mad enough to be **season ticket holders.** Most watch or listen from afar, taking the stick from their Cockney work mates (occasionally being able to dish it out) and countering the anti-northern **rubbish** from The London *Evening Standard*. Four times a year their award-winning magazine plops onto the doormat – cunningly titled 'mss' and edited by Julie Yates and Andy Smith – where alongside the many interviews you can see across these pages, the likes of **Harry Pearson,** Shaun Keogh, Claire Carvello, David Shayler and Steve Smith inform, amuse and inspire, where snappers Tim Hetherington and Paul Thompson illuminate with their **excellent** pictures, and where hard working club officials like Geoff Vickers, Jan Sanders, Paul Readman, Andy Walker and Gemma Roulston point members in the right direction for tickets, travel and **membership** fees. Nigel Pringle edits a cracking website **www.mss.org** which is essential surfing for *any* Boro fan. If you're **exiled from Teesside** or you know someone who is, it costs £15 a season to join. There's even a free diary...

A message from MSS President Wilf Mannion

I was delighted to be appointed Honorary President of Middlesbrough Supporters South in 1993, since when I have met some wonderful MSS people down in London at the MSS Annual Parties.

Both Albert Lanny and I greatly enjoy spending our Annual Party weekends with you truly wonderful supporters. I know the dedication many of you have in travelling thousands of miles a season to see the Boro play and let's hope it is all rewarded with a trophy or two in the not too distant future.

Good luck to Boro and especially to you all for 1999-2000. And last but not least congratulations MSS for reaching 25 years old!

---

mss issue 119 p20.
John Hendrie: "I was at the Old Trafford semi final, both Coca Cola cup finals and the FA Cup final, I'm prepared to give my weekends up to follow them. People have said it's great for me Barnsley going up and Boro going down but I don't think like that. I've got a feeling for the club, I want them to do really well."

mss issue 125 p 27 **Malcolm Allison:** "I knew I was going to get the sack because when the chairman asked for permission to sell the players I said NO. And he went and sold the players…"

mss issue 122, p33, **Gordon Jones** "When Graeme Souness signed, he was what we called a dicky dancer. He was a good passer but he was a prima donna… His first game was at Fulham and we nearly had fisticuffs in the dressing room. My legs were black and blue from the killer balls he was giving me. Jack Charlton told him if he didn't pull his socks up he was finished. He changed completely"

mss issue 114 p29
Alan Keen MP: "I had a go at John Major about Chelsea and he just took me apart completely by saying, *"Middlesbrough. Whenever I think of Middlesbrough I think of Wilf Mannion,"* he said".

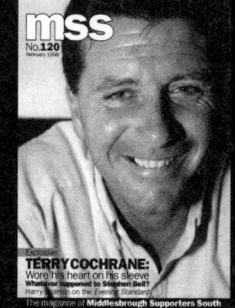

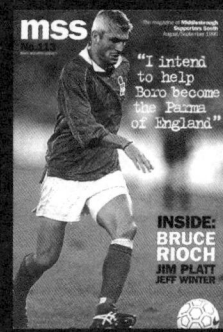

mss issue 116 p22
George Hardwick
"I think Middlesbrough would have won everything had the war not come because they had so many great players."

mss issue 123, p17, Alan Foggon:
(On that legendary story that he got a phone call in the Yellow Rose to report to the ground) "No, it was at Newport Working Mens Club. It was a match day but I wasn't playing or required to attend, so I used to go and have a game of snooker. The sub got injured so they needed another first team player and they knew where I was, so I got a phone call…"

mss issue 124, p20, David Shayler:
"It would have been typical if we had won the 1998 Coca Cola Cup final and picked up our first major honour when I absolutely couldn't be there as I was on the run from MI5…"

mss issue 104 p9 Steve Gibson:
"We said who do we want? Forget this football club and a hundred years of mediocrity, are we in business? Do we want it enough? And of course we did…"

mss issue 115 p14 Lennie Lawrence:
"I was the last of the old managers at Middlesbrough. I think I left Boro in an impeccable state: kids coming through, a small but decent standard of players by first Division standards. Robbo came and spent £3 million and got them up. That's fine but he couldn't have done it if the basis hadn't been there…"

mss issue 123, p28, John Hickton: "Every season we said: 'Two or more players and we'll be a great side'. They either didn't spend money or bought the wrong players. They say Jack had money but he would never spend it. Unlike Robson who has spent an unbelievable amount of money"

Join mss

■ To join MSS (£15 per season and £2 for any other member of the household) send your cheques, *made payable to MSS* to:
Jan Sanders, MSS Membership Secretary, 6 Valley Rise, Wheathampstead, Herts AL4 8JF.

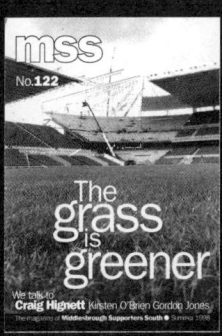

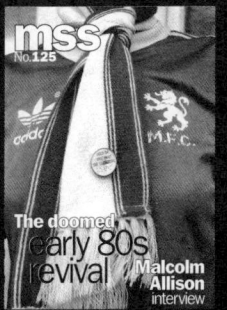

The FMTTM Millannual

G-R-E-A-T BORO MOMENTS

JOHN HENDRIE

The finest uncapped Scottish forward of all time. Whether on the wing or as central striker John Hendrie tore defences apart for Boro. Here we feature his legendary goal against Millwall Oct 13th 1990 - definitely not unlucky for Hendrie who ran the length of the field, cutting a swathe through the opposition before tucking the ball past the Millwall keeper infront of a disbelieving Holgate G-O-A-L!!

Players in the Moon

John Hendrie.
born 24/10/63, debut v West Ham 25/8/90. Last game 25/9/96 v Hereford.

WHAT DO YOU REMEMBER ABOUT YOUR FIRST GAME?

JH It was the first game of the season against West Ham on a very hot day. It was a drab 0-0 draw to be honest. West Ham were quite a good side so we were satisfied with a point. We were better away from home that season, because we were good on the counter. John Wark used to sit in front of the back four, break things up, and set us going. Whereas teams came to Ayresome Park and shut up shop, West Ham being a good example. We ended up losing to Notts County in the play offs.

WHAT DO YOU REMEMBER ABOUT YOUR LAST GAME?

JH I played in both legs of the Hereford cup tie. I came on at the Riverside, and set Curtis up for one of his few goals, we won 7-0. I played in the 2nd leg at Hereford, in the pouring rain. It was very heavy going, not the best place to go for a experienced professional. That was my last competitive game, but I played on the trip to Bangkok, shortly after that, scored a couple of goals and enjoyed the trip. The move to Barnsley happened as soon as we got back.

HOW ABOUT YOUR BEST MEMORY?

JH There's quite a few. The two promotions stand out. The first was at Wolves, although it was an awful game, it's always great to achieve promotion. Also the last game at Ayresome Park which all but clinched promotion. The atmosphere was terrific that day. There were a few lumps in the throat, tears in the eyes, I'll never forget that. When I go to Middlesbrough now I drive past the site to show my kids. People talk about the individual goals against Millwall and Norwich, they were smashing moments, but the last game against Luton is the one.

Happy memories.

MOONSTRUCK
Graham Gabriel

FIRST MATCH?

GG: Bill Gates Testimonial v Leeds United. I was 9 years old. I went in the Bob End with my friend's dad. Everyone lifted up off their seats when Boro scored, I just remember catching flashes of green between bodies.

BEST BORO MEMORY?

GG: The happiest was the atmosphere before the last match at Ayresome (v Luton).

WORST MEMORY?

The most emotional was when we got relegated last time around. I went to my local pub in Walthamstow, London, called Chequers and was really, really upset. I went home and the next morning (Monday) I got up for work, which was giving guided tours of London (for the Big Bus Sightseeing Tour) and I had a brand new driver. I got a coffee with her and bought a newspaper and saw the back page picture of Juninho on the ground in the centre circle and I started crying infront of the woman I had never seen before in my life. She said why are you so upset and I explained that this brilliant little Brazilian would now be leaving. She laughed at me and said I was daft.

We set off on tour and I thought I feel OK now, I can handle this. We came along Park Lane, and I was talking ".. this is Oxford Street on our left and this is Green Street where George Harrison and Ringo Starr used to live and there on your left is the Brazilian Embassy.." and I just burst into tears again.

After the tour the driver took me for a coffee. She said don't mention the Brazilian Embassy next time round.

So on the second tour of the day I went past it and saw the flag and didn't cry. Then we went through Mayfair and two very well dressed women got on. "Hello ladies," I said, "where are you from." With big beaming smiles they replied, "Brazil" and I started crying again.

The FMTTM Millannual

THE SHAPE OF THINGS TO COME

Nostalgia can be a terrible thing. In older fans it often mutates into a longing for the good old days when - as one reviewer of my biography of Boro legend Wilf Mannion put it - every team had a player called Wilf and England stuffed allcomers. But in thirtysomethings, like me, it becomes something far worse: a hankering after the good old, bad old days.

Remember them? The days, only a decade ago, when a season ticket cost something like sixty quid and when you and a gang of mates could roll up five minutes before kick-off and pay in - and when those kick-offs were almost all at 3pm on Saturdays. When your singing on the terraces was a key part of the team's efforts and goals were greeted with blurred roars, not Blur. And when the players had the same sort of Christian names as the crowd - Bernie, Gary or Stuart - rather than being called Christian, or Hamilton or Osvaldo.

Remember them as they really were? The facilities you endured for those cheap tickets and the not uncommon crushes at the turnstiles just before kick-off. When the some of the songs cascading from the terraces were as wretched as the safety standards which permitted great, unsafe surges to spill towards the pitch too. And when the standard of play could be so poor that Jan Molby seemed the epitome of continental elan.

But the good news for both those who pine for Old Football and new fans who were elsewhere 10 years ago is that one aspect of it seems to be returning. The only difficulty is that, as it is the empty spaces which used to be seen at every ground, neither group might actually be there to see it.

So far this season Spurs' opening game of the season was marred by swathes of empty seats, Sheffield Wednesday's attendances at the ground where the football revolution was conceived when 96 fans died in 1989 have tumbled and Aston Villa's manager and chairman have reportedly clashed over 12,000 unsold tickets when Boro visited Villa Park.

In response Villa dropped prices. Likewise, when I went to see Leeds play in the UEFA Cup a couple of months ago I paid £12 as the club tried to ensure a full house - for a side which is the fourth best in the country, pushing the really big boys at the top of the league and in Europe for the second year running.

The slump in attendances has prompted reports of the story many fans have been predicting for a time: the bursting of the bubble which has taken football from "a slum sport played in slum stadiums", according to the Sunday Times, to the richest league in the world; which has seen the sport move from the back pages of the newspapers to the front and saturation television coverage; and which has seen Boro move from Ayresome Park to the Riverside.

With England's disastrous Euro 2000 qualifying campaign - and the spectre of new TV battles and deals in which fans only ever lose, there's plenty to suggest that the gravy train might, just might, be heading for the sidings. And if that's the case, or whenever it eventually happens, get ready to see the blame to be apportioned on one group: greedy players.

But also remember two other things. In a nursing home in Redcar Wilf Mannion is seeing out his days with memories but no financial reward for his superb career. And that the villains of his story, and of the appalling standards at grounds in the 1970s and 80s and of the possible death by commercial exploitation of the 90s game are the same people: those who run the game.

Ten years ago in his epoch-making report on the Hillsborough disaster Lord Justice Taylor wrote: "In some instances it is legitimate to wonder whether the directors are genuinely interested in the welfare of their grass-roots supporters." Now, with the exception of chairmen such as Steve Gibson and Peter Ridsdale at Leeds who were fans long before they were businessmen and club directors, the same criticism applies. You only need to look at the empty seats to realise that.

* **Nick Varley** is author of **Parklife (Michael Joseph, £9.99)**, an examination of the football revolution since Hillsborough, and **Golden Boy, A Biography of Wilf Mannion (Aurum, £14.95)**.

c'mon, ref!

I've been thinking about all these changes that the authorities keep wanting to add to the game in order to install discipline or improve the <start American accent> entertainment quotient <stop American accent>. We've had the back pass rule, and the 6 second rule for keepers. We have seen experiments with kick-ins instead of throw-ins, with the rugby style 10 yard penalty for hassling the ref and now there is talk about introducing another "egg chasers" innovation, playing advantage for ages (and ages) before dragging everyone back for something that everyone else had forgotten about. This last one, I feel, is bound to work against the Boro. Can you imagine it, 4-0 up against Newcastle with 2 minutes to go, when the referee, one Mr G. Eordie-Bustard, brings the game back to the kick-off as one of our players may have been encroaching the centre circle. It's just not going to work is it. More importantly, I feel is a law to prevent the following sort of situation.

The game is well underway. The opposition midfield general (for the sake of clarity we shall call him Dennis Thighs) has dished out enough punishment to earn employee of the month at the Linda Whiplash "House of Pain" massage parlour (it's on Borough Rd). Although Thighs was booked after 3 minutes for introducing one of our players to the thrill of "bungee free" bungee jumping (our lad was subsequently booked for descent) he has spent the rest of the game attempting to create gainful employment for the local Accident & Emergency ward. The referee, playing the counter role of Walter the Softy to perfection, is completely in Dennis' thrall, to the point where he agreed to book our keeper for diving even though he was trying to save a penalty at the time. I'm sure you will all agree this is an all too common scenario, which needs addressing at the earliest opportunity. We need to develop a method for countering these persistent foulers and I think I may just have hit upon the solution. How does this sound?

For every foul committed a player has to wear another article of clothing!

Hang on, before you move on to the next article, let it sink in for a while. It's deceptively simple, yet devilishly cunning. The worse the offence, the bigger and more outlandish the gear they must don. A tug on the shirt would be rewarded with a Fair Isle sweater. A deliberate trip would see the offending player slipping into a pair of "swish-swish" flares straight out of 1975. The type the trendy, acne riddled youth on the "Tomorrow People" used to wear. (Incidentally, how wrong was *that* program? Mind you it wasn't as off the mark as Space "Mmmm nice shiny shirt, pass me another blue drink" 1999 was. What *were* they thinking? They imagined Moon Bases and we got Center Parks).

Dissent would be rewarded with one of those big, whole head, horror masks. You know the ones, with the patented Real Looking Nylon Hair effect and Genuine Fake Painted on Blood. Kicking the ball away would mean a big pair of yellow clown boots with red laces and two footed tackles might lead to the offender hopping around madly in a sack. Especially frustrating for Arsenal's defenders who would be bouncing around desperately holding up the sack with one hand and appealing for offside with he other.

Goalkeepers that have fouled would be tethered to a pole 10 yards to the right of the goal using an 8 yard length of heavy duty elastic rope, so that they have to time the gathering of crosses to perfection, collecting the ball just at the limit of the ropes elasticity, or risk being spronged (Don't look it up. I just invented it) back at a ridiculous pace, clutching thin air and possibly wiping out a few defenders as an added bonus.

Each subsequent offence would have the rope shortened until the only tactic left open to them would be to desperately claw their way to the far post and wrap all their limbs around it. Thus anchored in place, the thick elastic rope vibrating with tension, they would wait for a goal bound effort and time letting go to perfection. Within a fractions of a second they would be whizzing across the goalmouth at 1,000 miles per hour hopefully gathering the ball as they go. I feel this could lead to some astonishingly impressive saves. The sort of saves Steve Pears used to pull off on a weekly basis.

At the end of an hour or so, those niggley, annoying, shirt pulling, trip-and-run merchants would be staggering around the park under 20 layers of clothing, doing great big Coco the Clown moon-walk steps in their three foot long boots, effectively rendering them harmless. After a particularly nasty game we might see half the players sporting Frankenstein, Dracula and "Curse of the Mummy" masks frantically running around bumping into each other in a sort of "International It's a Knockout" for the undead.

Even better, occasionally goalkeepers would be catapulted out of the stadium as elastic rope, already under enormous strain, eventually gives with an impressive "twangggg" sound. I can only see it as being of huge benefit to the game and lets face it, if John Barnes' attire when Sky's expert summariser is anything to go by, some players are already voluntarily dressing in a hugely amusing manner.

I'm sure you will all agree this is a solution that will work, is enforceable, requires no great technological innovations and will prove hours of fun as we watch Mark Bosnich disappear into the Tees with an ever diminishing wail and a dull splash.

Works for me.

Jon Todd

Marooned on Moon Island

ERIC PAYLOR

FIVE MATCH VIDEOS

I'd love to see videos of the great games which took place many years before I was born.
1 Boro 2, Sunderland 3 - September 12, 1903. The inaugural match at Ayresome Park. What a match it must have been in front of a packed 30,000 stadium. And the young Tim Williamson was in goal for Boro.
2 Boro 10, Sheffield United 3 - Goals galore. Boro's highest league score, and George Camsell scored four. Billy Brown, Bobby Stuart, Bobby Bruce. Great names from yesteryear. Yet the crowd was only 6,461. Shame.
3 Boro 9, Blackpool 2 - December 10, 1938. Wilf Mannion scored four, and Mickey Fenton three. Other internationals included Bob Baxter and Jack Milne. This is the team they reckoned would have won the league but for the war.
4 Boro 1, Burnley 1 - March 1, 1946. More than 53,000 packed into Ayresome Park for the sixth round clash in the FA Cup. Thousands more were locked outside. Maybe this game generated the best ever atmosphere at Ayresome Park.
5 Charlton Athletic 6, Boro 6 - October 22, 1960. Whenever Brian Clough scored at one end, Boro threw one in at the other. This would have been an experience to tell the grandchildren about.

WHAT COULDN'T YOU DO WITHOUT?
My pen.

BORO MANAGER FRIDAY
Willie Maddren. If the island was truly enchanted, he would never have contracted his horrendous illness.

The FMTTM Millannual

The FMTTM Millannual

1970 and all that

by Robert Shrug

Foot-Warming Flares, Footballing Flair...

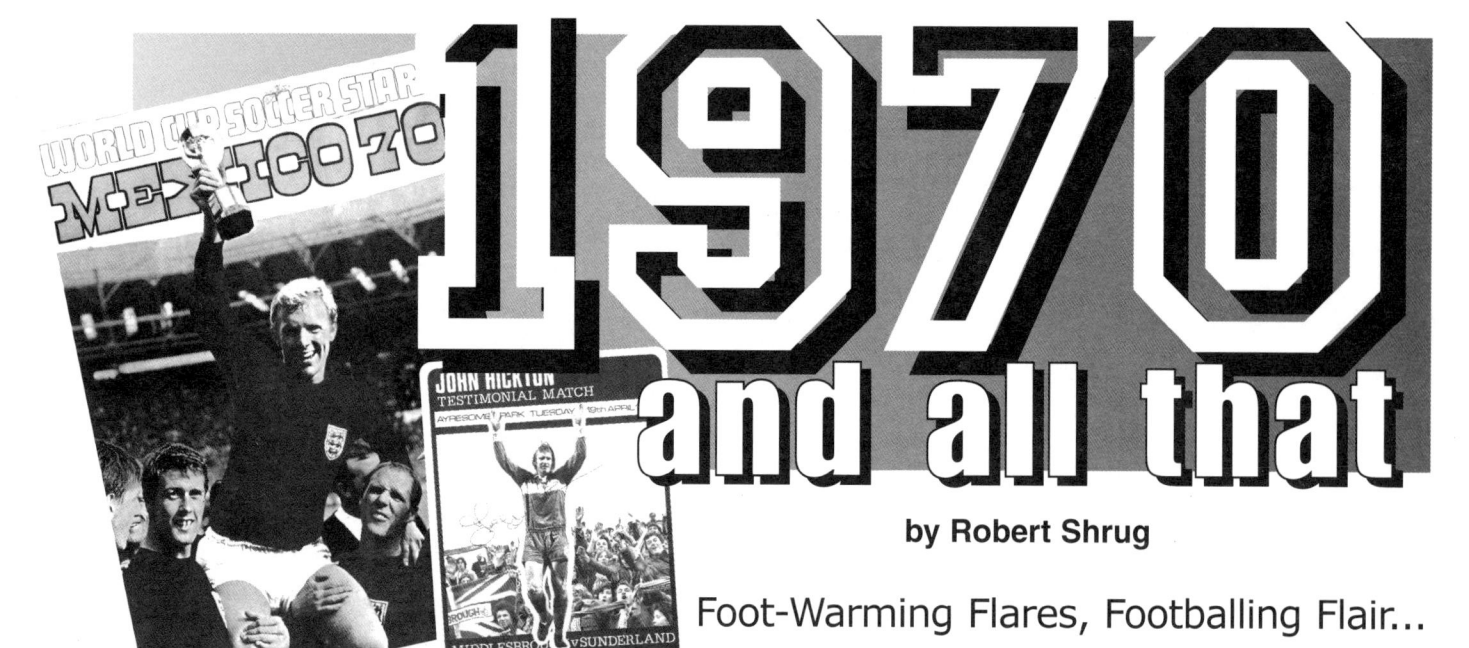

This year I had my 37th birthday, I was going to say celebrated but 'mourned' might be more apposite. Imagine that, 37 years. I'm now even past the veteran age for footballers, I'm now deep into what Ian Cusack once christened as "Naff off Granddad" territory. You know, the brain's still going strong but the legs aren't quite up to speed. Alright I suppose I could still be a player-coach of an ambitious, underachieving second division outfit. Or to look on an even brighter side I could be a young manager just stepping out of a tracksuit into a houndstooth sports jacket and hopping onto the first rung of the managerial whirly-gig. Yes I like the sound of that, 'young' manager. I'll use that football comparison from now on.

Sorry about that bit of meandering self-indulgence, I suppose I've maybe jumped ahead of myself a bit. But, correct me if I'm wrong, doesn't everyone go through life with a football calendar ticking away in the background? Don't you measure your every passing year against those notched up by your footballing stars? When you were 18 or 19 you were almost like a born again bairn, you could easily have been a hot junior prospect knocking on the first team door, like an Andy Campbell, a Jamie Pollock or in my case a Mark Proctor or a Craig Johnston. A few years later you could easily have been playing for the national under-21 side and that means you are still officially a youngster. At the age of 23 you sought consolation in the

Billy Woof was the hottest youth prospect at Boro for so long he almost earned a testimonial

recent past, David Mills had been a young - there's that word again - star of England under-23s. At the age of 24 Mikkel Beck was still being described as one for the future, at Derby County. Billy Woof was the hottest youth prospect at Boro for so long he almost earned a testimonial. Boro's oldest young pretender finally made his make or break through at the age of 26! At which age Archie Stephens was still working in the real world, he hadn't even laced his boots for his Football League bow at Bristol Rovers. So at 26 you could still have the whole of your (footballing) life infront of you. Nice to know.

Anyway, as I face up to the Neville Southall "fat of the land" years at least I have one great consolation from which to draw comfort. I was old enough to watch and understand the greatest World Cup tournament of all time, Mexico 1970. And you can't take that away from me, well not until the onset of senility or as the result of the after effects of BSKYB Premiership brainwash. But anyway you young pups and scamps out there I can well remember crowding around a crackling black'n'white TV before school to decipher the fuzzy satellite pictures winging their way all the way from central America. Pele, Gerson, Felix, Banks, Charlton and Bobby Moore. Me and my mates would be out playing football across the back field and discussing Bank's wonder save against Brazil. We would then conduct a swaps session for the Esso World Cup coins, and talk would turn to the first coin, Leeds full back Paul Reaney who had broken his leg before the tournament. We would devise strategies on how to get the rare Peter Shilton coin, it was rumoured Mark Wheater down the road had one but no one was too certain. In the end some older lad Magee from over near Captain Cook's came up with the goods albeit with a size eight Tuff shoe stamp right across Shilloggs chops. Turns out he'd deliberately stamped on the face taken it back to the garage as defective and had the cheek to persuade the attendant open all the sealed paper bags until he found another Shilton, then he traded the damaged goods with me and my brother.

It's all coming flooding back to me now. Yes, when the Tonibell ice cream van tinkered down the street we'd rush across to buy screwballs to toast our soccer heroes. I had a pre-Panini sticker of my hero, the greatest overlapping left back of all time, TC, Terry Cooper. Four years later this world class England star would join Middlesbrough as a replacement for Frank Spraggon and I couldn't believe it. Although he'd been out with a broken leg for an absolute age, wasn't it about two years? Cooper had made a full recovery and even played a half for England (although no doubt having Don Revie as national boss was a bit of a help in his selection).

But even so it was an unbelievable signing for Boro, our first household name since Bobby Murdoch (who was always more famed north of the border) or the veteran Nobby Stiles. Suddenly we had a world class superstar in our ranks, a ticket for the Boro entitled you to watch Terry Cooper playing on our scared turf alongside everyone's Boro idol Big John Hickton.

It' disappointing to me how seldom Terry Cooper's name crops up when people discuss their greatest ever Boro teams. For Boro's first TC, and the original super Cooper was soon back to his brilliant England best, ripping teams apart with his storming runs down the flank. A drop of the shoulder, a shimmy, a feint and TC was away with his marker trailing in his wake. What value Cooper today? In this the age of the wing-back Boro had arguably the greatest ever exponent of the art of the overlap. He must have been pretty good at swearing as well, dismissed at Chelsea for uttering profanities at a linesman. Although in all he only notched one goal in his 100+ appearances with Terry Cooper and Spike Armstrong Boro had perhaps the deadliest left side in the league.

Had Big Jack been more ambitious on the trail of quality strikers then we must surely have added considerably to that solitary Anglo-Scottish prize.

Anyway, there you have it, for all the other oldies out there, the advantages of being 37 years of age are many. We were there for Mexico 1970 (well in front of the telly at any rate), we watched with mother through Pogul's Wood and Bill and Ben. We saw Paulus the Wood Gnome, Robert's Robots and remember Pete Purvis in Dr Who (just about). And we had Terry Cooper in our team. Mind you I'm still left completely mystified by "The Singing Ringing Tree."

marooned on moon island
HARRY PEARSON

FIVE MATCH VIDEOS

1 v Carlisle United 1967
The first game I ever went to, I was six. We won 4-0, but I didn't see any of the goals. We went home at half-time because we couldn't get a seat in the Bob End and standing in the Holgate made my legs ache. I was tough even in those days. John O'Rourke got a hat-trick.
2 v Sheffield Wednesday 1974 - 8-0. What more do you need to know.
3 Blackburn Rovers 1987 - I really enjoyed the football we played under Rioch. This was a classic Boxing Day game: packed ground, smell of after-shave etc. It finished 1-1.
4 v Leeds United 1992 - 4-1. I think the result that gave me the greatest pleasure ever. Whatever happened to Tommy Wright?
5 v West Ham 1995 - Just to see Juninho, especially the moment when he wrestled Julian Dicks to the ground.

MEMORABILIA
A recording of that *"It's nice to know you're here"* song which always made me laugh (even though it's not big, or clever to swear)

BORO PERSON
Paul Merson. Because then everyone else on the planet would be spared having to listen to him.

FIRST MATCH
That Carlisle game.

BEST MEMORY
Portsmouth away in 1990 with MSS. Good pub, good company and Gary Stevens scored in his own net.

WORST MEMORY
The club sliding into oblivion during 1985-86 at the same time that my grandfather, who'd first taken me to watch them, was slowly dying from the effects of a stroke.

WHAT A "TO DO" AT HALF TIME

It has always been a major struggle to survive those terrible minutes, when time seems to stop and life begins to lose all meaning, in spite of the best efforts of the establishment. Half time entertainment at the Riverside has often been anything but in the eyes of the not-so appreciative members of the crowd; those not partaking in the poisoning of body and mind that is the Concourse Experience.

The club has tried it's level best, apart from a change from Mark Page, to provide alternatives to the contemplation of the first half or one's navel, with the latter being the more interesting during the majority of last seasons home games. We have had the "penalty" competition, about which most people cannot find a bad thing to say, where the local kids take advantage of the full sized goals and the half size keepers to score the most goals.

Presumably, in the old days, this was done with a wet "casey" whereupon the ball travelled far more slowly, giving the keeper a chance to get to it. Unfortunately its momentum was such that the poor lad would have to be carried off on a stretcher if foolish enough to get between the net and the striker. In later years, with the "plastic" balls, it has been a source of constant wonder that the ball has evaded the net on so many occasions. Still the hilarity factor was always present and those with a personal interest could engage in a bit of barracking to put the striker or the goalkeeper off. Even better the club could reinforce its involvement with the local community creating mutual goodwill all round.

With equal hilarity, the "fan quiz" was a hit in it's own way. Marvelling at the prowess, or more often the lack of it, of the contestants, and wondering what made them get out there in the first place. The inclusion of the away fans, who, being dedicated enough to find Middlesbrough in the first place, generally win, means that we can maintain the rivalry and laugh together as well. The fact that the bag of "Boro goodies" is dumped in the waste bin of the first Service Station the coach stops at is neither here nor there.

Without doubt the strangest, and most courageous, was the introduction of "culture" to the interval, and this does not include the delicious food lurking in the smog downstairs. It could be argued that we were being softened up by the introduction of the "classical" music at the start of the match, especially on the flag days, but few were prepared for the sights and sounds that included Opera singers, violinists, folk singers and dance troupes. This was akin to Alan Hansen doing a commentary on the dancers in Swan Lake from a footballing perspective. "Well there was no need for the swan to die there, the other guy was clearly offside and the conductor should have spotted it straight away rather than waiting for the first violinist to raise his bow". Obviously playing as safe as they could the performers have been kept in front of the relatively mild West Stand, when was the last time we heard them chanting? Even so the poor sods from the Folk band got a fair amount of stick, after about the seventh verse and chorus.

Despite the vocal reception of the new entertainment, it offered a taste of otherwise ignored fare and it gave the good burghers of Middlesbrough an opportunity to appreciate the bio-diversity of talent that emanates from Teesside. Personally having never had any interest in "folk" music it was interesting to be subjected to a very small interlude to decide whether it may become part of my general listening. The fact that it was both far better than I expected and reinforced some of my preconceptions of the harmonies, and length of the songs, did me no harm at all, though I did not feel any need to listen to any more. To the open minded this was easy education that could be ignored if so desired. I congratulate the club, the organisers and the brave artistes who tried their very best. It made a change.

So this season we will be subjected to entertainment that will be of interest to some and not to others. You cannot please all of the crowd all of the time, but provided it does not impinge upon reading the wit and wisdom contained within FMTTM, (Donkeywatch is obviously excluded by that description), who really cares?

Mark Coupe

marooned on moon island

DAVID SHAYLER

To all intents and purposes, I might as well live on a desert island. After all, I'm as capable of watching the Boro play in Bora Bora as I am exiled in France. Still, I should be thankful for small mercies. At least, now that I'm out of prison, I can see live games on Sky in the pub and listen to live commentary on Century Radio via the Internet. This arrangement is not ideal but it is better than the coverage I had in prison. For the first three months of last season, I had to wait until ten o'clock Sunday evening to get the result, which came via Canal+, a French TV channel, showing the premier league round-up. It was usually all over in about ten seconds. But at least I got to see the goals.

People think I'm making it up when I say that the only thing I really miss about the UK is not watching the Boro play. But it's true. I've always seen going to a Boro match as a kind of therapy as it's an excuse to:

• Talk about the Boro non-stop with my brothers on the four-hour journey up from London.

• Release all the pent-up frustration that builds up during a normal week at work by abusing the ref and/or Joe Bolton/Jimmy Phillips/Brian Deane or whoever else has the honour of being our latest whipping boy.

• Go out and get legless with that warm glow of victory inside (I always hope).

Everything else I miss about the UK -- friends and family, good telly, brown sauce -- can either come to me or be accessed through the global media.

I must be the only person -- apart from a few money-grabbing chairmen -- who can't wait for the advent of pay per view. At least come 3 o'clock Saturday afternoon, I'd be able to pull up a chair, crack open a beer and settle down to the nearest I could get to the match-day experience.

FIVE MATCH VIDEOS

The 1996/97 FA Cup run
(without the final)

The reasons for choosing this are obvious. After the defeat in the 6th round replay against Wolves in 81, I spent much of my life aching for another FA Cup quarter final. But for many years (with the exception of 1992) our presence in the sixth round of the world's oldest football competition seemed about as likely as the second coming. So when we beat Man City in the fifth round in 97, I just knew I had to be there for the sixth round against Derby County. I rate that match as the greatest Middlesbrough game of all time. When Rav unleashed that left foot screamer in the 89th minute, all I remember is the whole world going into slow motion as 4,000 Boro fans watched the ball head goalwards for what seemed like an eternity.

The next thing I knew the ball was nestling in the net and I was hugging the stranger who had the misfortune to be standing next to me as 121 years of bad luck, awful refereeing and abject failure were finally laid to rest. Even then, I spent the three or four minutes of injury time hoping they didn't sneak a consolation goal and put the pressure back on us, causing us to make unforced errors in defence leading to horror of horrors the inevitable Derby equaliser. Fortunately, my capacity for paranoia exceeded the Boro's capacity for snatching defeat from the jaws of victory -- for once.

Of course, we then demonstrated all that has made us the club we know and love in the semi-final, a game I was at but watched through my fingers rather in the way that I watched Dr Who, as a kid. Now, it's over I can laugh with everyone else outside Teesside at what must have been the greatest ever FA Cup semi-final but at the time, it was an exhausting, white-knuckle rollercoaster ride.

Even the replay was memorable and not just because we won and went to our first FA Cup final. It remains in the memory for the Juninho goal that never was, the goal that appeared as 'Middlesbrough 2 Chesterfield 0' on the Hillsborough scoreboard but later disappeared without comment. At the time, I argued with my brother that it had been disallowed. He even thought of trying to phone a friend to confirm the scoreline but didn't have his mobile on him. That would have to be a first phoning a friend to find out the score of a match we were at. I've since seen the TV coverage. It shows that the Sky team, Andy Gray included, were fooled as well. I think they only realised just before half time that there was still, as they say, everything to play for.

Mind you, I felt most sorry for the bloke sitting behind us. About midway through the second half with the score still at 1-0. He said: "Thank God, we got that second," only to be met by a stares of disbelief. I explained to him that it was in fact 1-0 and we were by no means definitely on our way to our first FA Cup Final.

I bought the video to the final when it came out. I've even tried to watch it a couple of times. But I can never get past the half hour mark. Once Mustoe and Rav had limped off, we would have been better off conceding the match there and then. It would have saved us all a load of hassle.

Man Utd v Boro, Premier League, 19 December 1998

Quite the most remarkable result in living memory, as David Coleman might say. By a fluke, I caught the goals the evening of the match on some Eurosatellite channel. I saw them again recently on a video of *They Think It's All Over*. It was sent to me by a Boro fan because it showed Bernie Slaven eating his words -- or rather baring his bum in Binns window -- as a result of a rash but entirely rational prediction that we had no chance, made before the game. If the club haven't released this as a one-off video, they're not serious about merchandising.

Boro v Man City, Division 1, 21st September 1974

My first game. This one's not on video but I wish it was. I seem to remember Millsy scored in the first half from about 40 yards but it probably only looked that far because I was eight. Strangely, I have a better recollection of City's Willie Donaghie being sent off for punching John Hickton but that's probably because in those days I understood the intricacies of a good fight rather than the subtlety of good football. Mind you, I don't think the Charlton era is remembered for "sexy" football, as it would be called today. The Boro's hard, unrelentingly cynical style was so well-known that the day's leading sitcom character, Norman Stanley Fletcher, got a few laughs at the expense of us and our football team, in an episode of *Porridge*.

1991/92 season review

This remains with me as one of Boro's greatest seasons, partly because we had two good cup runs and got promoted and partly because it was the first time I saw more than half the games in a season. The video goes on for hours from what I remember and there are some supreme Middlesbrough moments like:
a. Bernie scoring against Sunderland after 17 seconds.
b. Gittens and Wilko scoring in the last 15 minutes of the season to send us up when we were 1-0 down and reduced to ten men.
c. Pally in a Man Utd shirt clearing the ball off the line towards the end of normal time in the semi-final of the Rumbelows Cup when the score stood at 1-1.

I've often wondered what went through Pally's mind in that moment. It's the kind of mad fantasy cum nightmare that often went through my mind when I was a kid: what would I do if I made it as a professional footballer but finished up playing for the opposition against the Boro in an FA Cup quarter final? I concluded that I would quietly slip one -- or two or three, if that were necessary --past my own keeper to secure us that coveted and historic semi-final place. Pally obviously didn't concur although I still think he could have slipped over in the Old Trafford mud, making the whole thing look like an accident, while allowing the ball to squelch its way over the line and the Boro to go to Wembley for the first time. I ask you; what the hell did he want with a Rumbelows Cup Winners medal, anyway? I mean, he'd already won a Cup Winners' Cup final with Utd.

Marooned STILL on moon island
DAVID SHAYLER

FIVE MATCH VIDEOS

Boro's greatest goals

This is supposed to be a collection of Boro's greatest goals as chosen by the fans. Some of the goals would be hard pushed to make it into a collection of Hartlepool's greatest moments, though. It may be great to remember the days that Boro players scored hat tricks against Arsenal but I hardly think that a 1977 five yard tap-in by David Mills with the keeper already beaten and the net empty can ever qualify as one of the greatest 150 goals the Boro have ever scored. That said, this tape has tremendous sentimental value. Chris Joseph, a one-armed Boro fan who now acts as my agent, brought it over with a load of pies just after I got out of prison so it was the first Boro action I saw after my release. It also has tonnes of my favourite Boro goals on, like:

a. Jamie Pollock's 35-yard screamer against Leicester in 1992, which was also his first for the club.
b. Ravanelli's 20-yard left footer against Derby in the sixth round which, unlike the version on The Road to Wembley tape, is accompanied by an epic commentary from the immortal Mottie befitting the occasion.
c. The only Boro goal ever scored at Wembley, which should have given us our first trophy in 121 years.
d. John Hendrie's tantalising 90-yard dribble and clinical finish v Millwall in 1991, which reminds me of that Maradona goal against England in the 1986 World Cup.

MEMORABILIA

If I had a woman with me, I would take the Boro suspenders and panties (although they have sadly been deleted from the club catalogue) so she could wear them all the time because I'm like that. (I'm not making this up. In the 1994/95 season, fans were offered a suspender belt and panties covered in hundreds of tiny club crests and the legend: "I scored at Ayresome Park"). As I'll probably be spending my time with Bernie Slaven (see below) and I've already seen him in a skirt on telly (see above), I'd probably opt for last season's away shirt, again for sentimental and personal reasons. I wore it on the maddest day of life, the day that I walked free from prison.

BORO PERSON

As I said above, I'd probably go with Bernie Slaven since unlike other commentators, he actually seems to know what he is talking about. I've never met him but he also strikes me as the sort of bloke who has a sense of humour and he's always been one of my Boro heroes, despite the totally unjustified criticism he used to get at the Boro. I sometimes wonder if he has the best goals per £ ratio in the modern game. I mean, he cost us about £25,000 in an age of £million players and is still one of the most prolific strikers in the history of the club. And he is that rare thing -- a teetotal Scotsman/Irishman so he'd also keep me off the piss, should we ever come across fermenting coconut or whatever on this desert island. Oh yeah, and I would also like to ask him what it's like to be mentioned in a Booker Prize-winning novel, as he was -- in The Van by Roddy Doyle. For those of you who don't know, The Van covered the exploits of Irish fans travelling to the 1990 World Cup. At one point, the novel runs through the entire Republic of Ireland squad, of which Bernie was a member.

The FMTTM Millannual

marooned on moon island
JEFF BROWN - TYNE TEES

FIVE MATCHES

i) Boro v Liverpool, first game of 96-97 season. Rav hat-trick. What a way to start the season.
ii) Boro v Newcastle, Coca-cola Cup, same season. Unbelievable atmosphere. Unbelievable result.
iii) Boro v Liverpool, Coca-Cola Cup semi-final 2nd leg. Branca's arrival. Another unforgettable night.
iv) Boro v Everton, FA Cup 4th round reply, 87-88. One of THE great Cup ties. Any game featuring Cloughie. Heard so much about him from my dad, would love to be able to see more than the odd snippets that survive.

MEMORY/MEMORABILIA

The bomb site - masquerading as the staff car park - that we have to wade through to get to every game at the Riverside. Home games just wouldn't be the same without it...

BORO PERSON

David Hodgson. Saw him climb into the Holgate before a match once (West Brom FA Cup tie, 1981, I think), standing with the fans because he was suspended. Thought he was a good bloke then - haven't changed that opinion since I've met him.

G-R-E-A-T BORO MOMENTS

Hickton's penalty run up.... getting closer

MOONSTRUCK

FIRST EVER BORO GAME?

I know you said the first one you can properly remember but I have trouble remembering my own name let alone various football matches. It amazes me reading the interviews when you reminisce about incidents in different matches. I only hope that my daughters don't inherit this lack of memory.

Anyway the first game I went to was at Ayresome Park and was against Derby County, (my Grandad's team and it was he and my father who took my brother and I). It was a birthday present so it must have been December-ish, and because they had been promoted it was probably 1975. The pitch was wet, but it was not actually raining just darkish, we were sat a few rows up from the pitch not far from the halfway line in the West Stand. I remember the left back pounding up the touchline in the mud. We lost, 2-0 I think, and my Grandad said it was not a good game, but I enjoyed it. I remember how fast we left the ground and walking at a breakneck pace to leave the vicinity before any "trouble" started.

BEST BORO MOMENT?

When the Boro team came onto the pitch for the Coca Cola Cup Final I was in tears. I was filled with the same pride and happiness that I had felt when my daughters were born. Even thinking about it brings a lump to my throat.

WORST BORO MOMENT?

When Leicester City equalised in the CCCF. I had been screaming at Boro to get the ball in the corners and play possession. Instead they went for glory and reaped disaster. So easily avoided, obvious to even the tiniest footballing brain, the equaliser took away all my hopes for the Boro. Even now my stomach clenches at the memory. I do not think we will ever have a better chance.

Mark Coupe

Marooned on Moon Island

**MIKE AMOS
NORTHERN ECHO**

MY FAVOURITE FIVE

Oldham Athletic 5 Shildon 2 - November 4 1961. We scored first - George Sinclair header, I can still see it. It was bonfire night, no M62 so fish and chips and the green 'un in Leeds and still the last time Shildon reached the FA Cup first round.

Arsenal 2 Liverpool 1 - FA Cup final, May 5 1971. The double, Charlie George flat out and a young lady from Derbyshire alongside. Canny day, canny night.

Liverpool 0 Arsenal 2 - May 1989. Unable to watch, I'd hidden away in one of the few pubs I know with neither television nor interest in football. The big bairn was barely eight, stayed at home and broke down crying. It's up for grabs now - and still brings a moist eye, the most fantastic finish ever.

North Ferriby 0 Whitby 3 - Carlsberg FA Vase final, May 10 1997. Victory at Wembley in my first season as Northern League chairman - royal box and all that - and a chance meeting with the Arnott Insurance man whose company now so generously sponsors the League.

Catterick Cubs 0 Richmond Dundas Cubs 1 - some time in 1994. Dundas had never won the six-a-side cup, their winner a 15 yard shot aimed inch perfect inside the post. The little 'un scored it - by far the greatest goal the world has ever seen.

Fly me to the Moon is the official "Unofficial" voice of the Boro. Now in its 12th season FMTTM was voted fanzine of the year 1998/99 by the Telegraph.

Editorial Address:
FMTTM,
Unit 7, Brentnall Centre,
Brentnall St,
Middlesbrough
TS1 5AP

Tel: 01642/249696
Fax: 01642/247878
Email: fmttm@onyexnet.co.uk